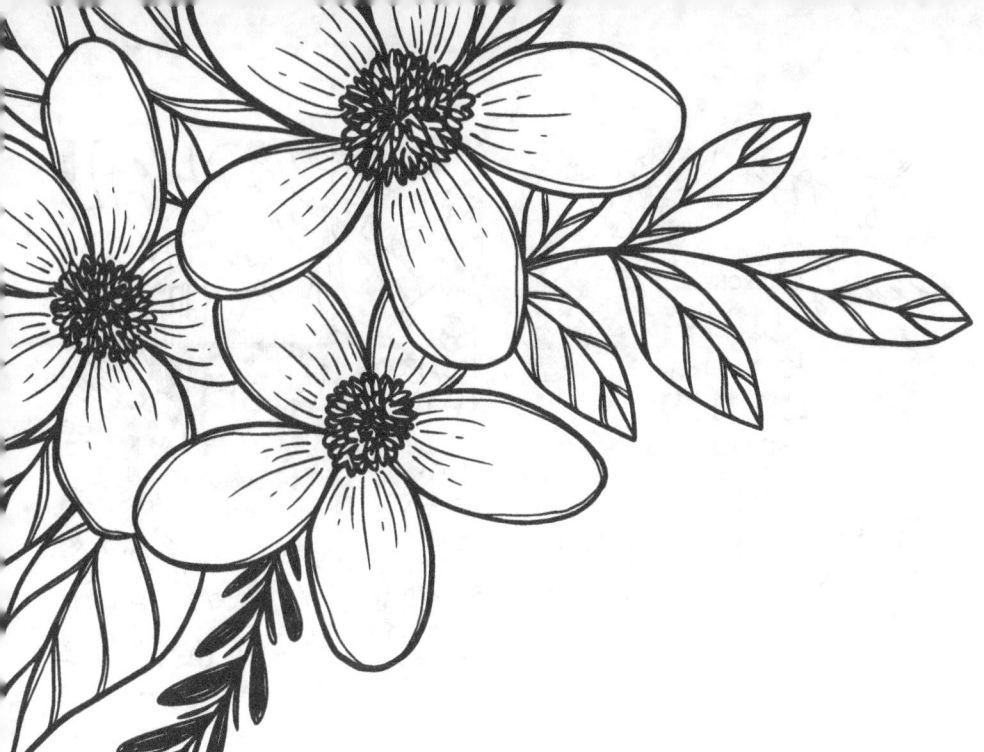

This Bible Verse

Coloring Book Belongs To

_____

_____

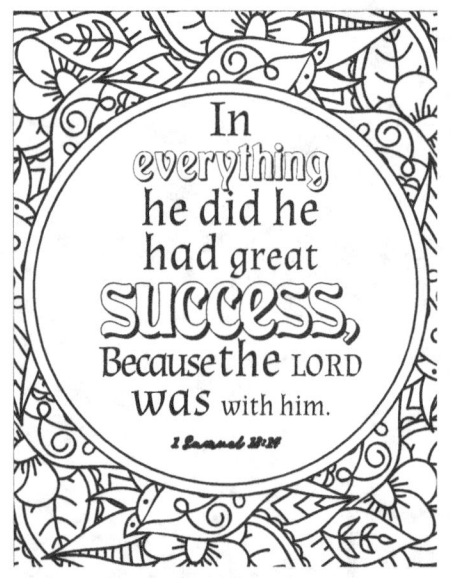

In everything he did he had great **SUCCESS**, Because the LORD was with him.

1 Samuel 18:14

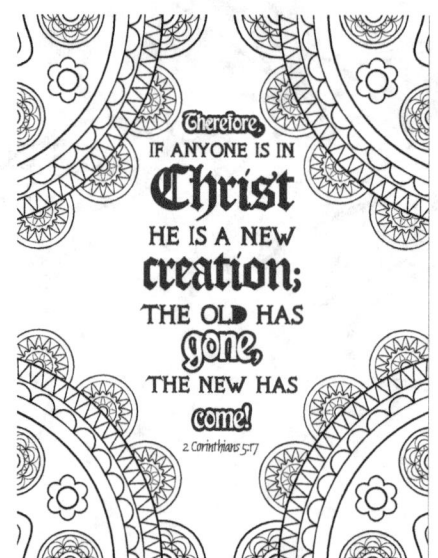

Therefore, IF ANYONE IS IN **Christ** HE IS A NEW **creation**; THE OLD HAS **gone**, THE NEW HAS **come!**

2 Corinthians 5:17

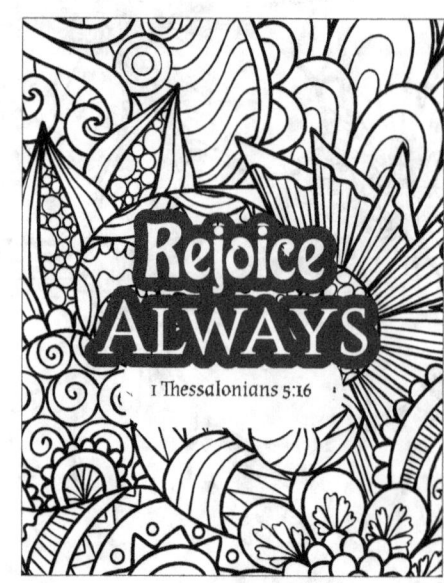

Rejoice ALWAYS

1 Thessalonians 5:16

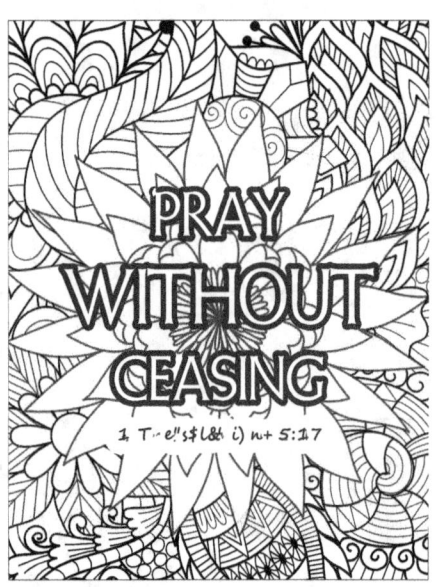

PRAY WITHOUT CEASING

1 Thessalonians 5:17

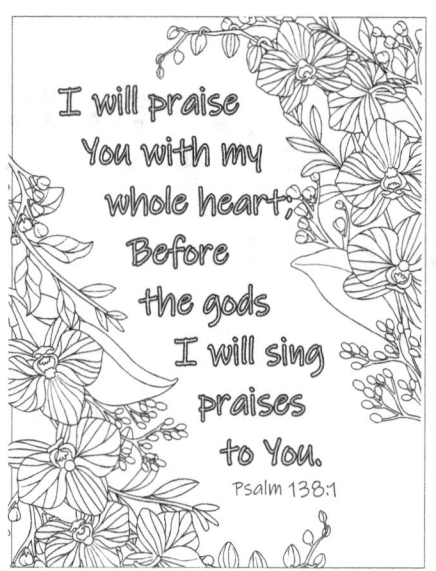

I will praise You with my whole heart; Before the gods I will sing praises to You.

Psalm 138:1

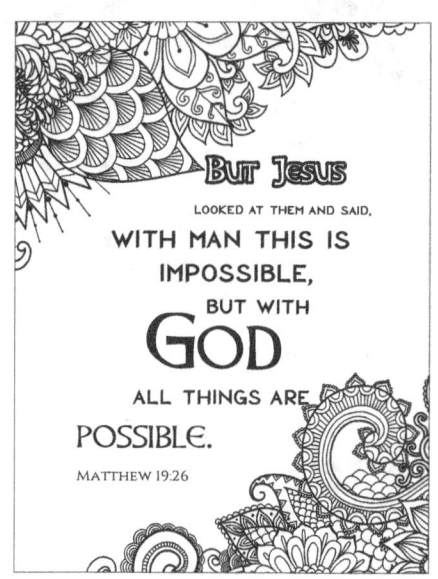

But Jesus LOOKED AT THEM AND SAID, WITH MAN THIS IS IMPOSSIBLE, BUT WITH **GOD** ALL THINGS ARE POSSIBLE.

MATTHEW 19:26

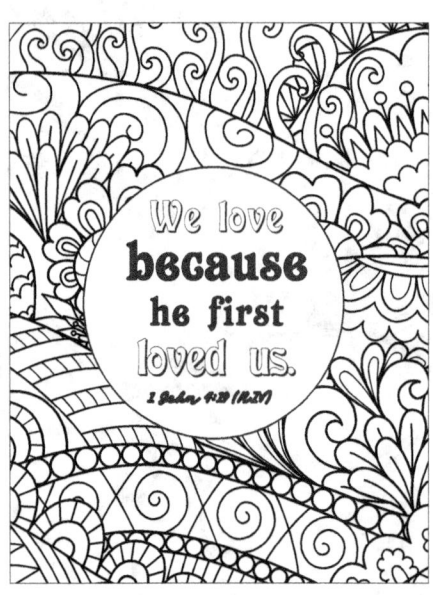

We love **because** he first loved us.

1 John 4:19 (NIV)

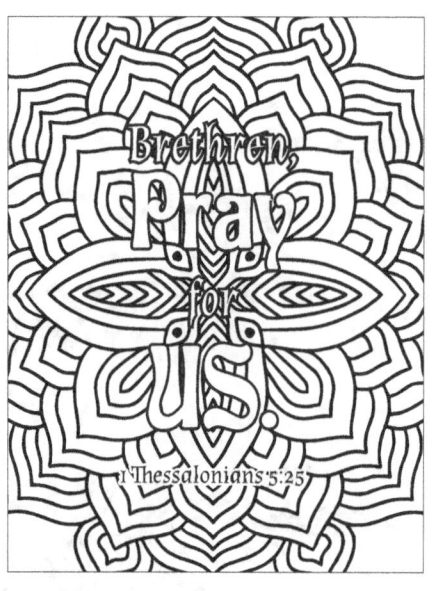

Brethren, **Pray** for **us.**

1 Thessalonians 5:25

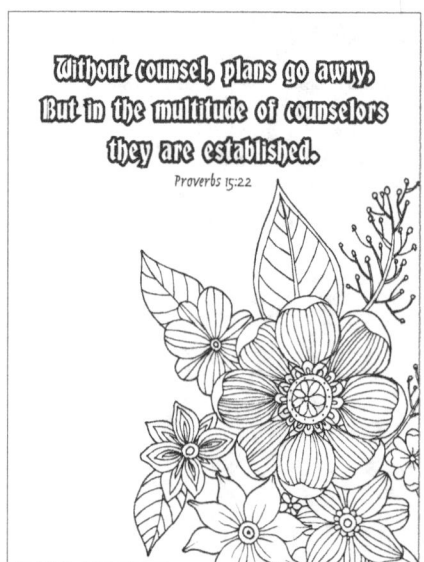

Without counsel, plans go awry, But in the multitude of counselors they are established.

Proverbs 15:22

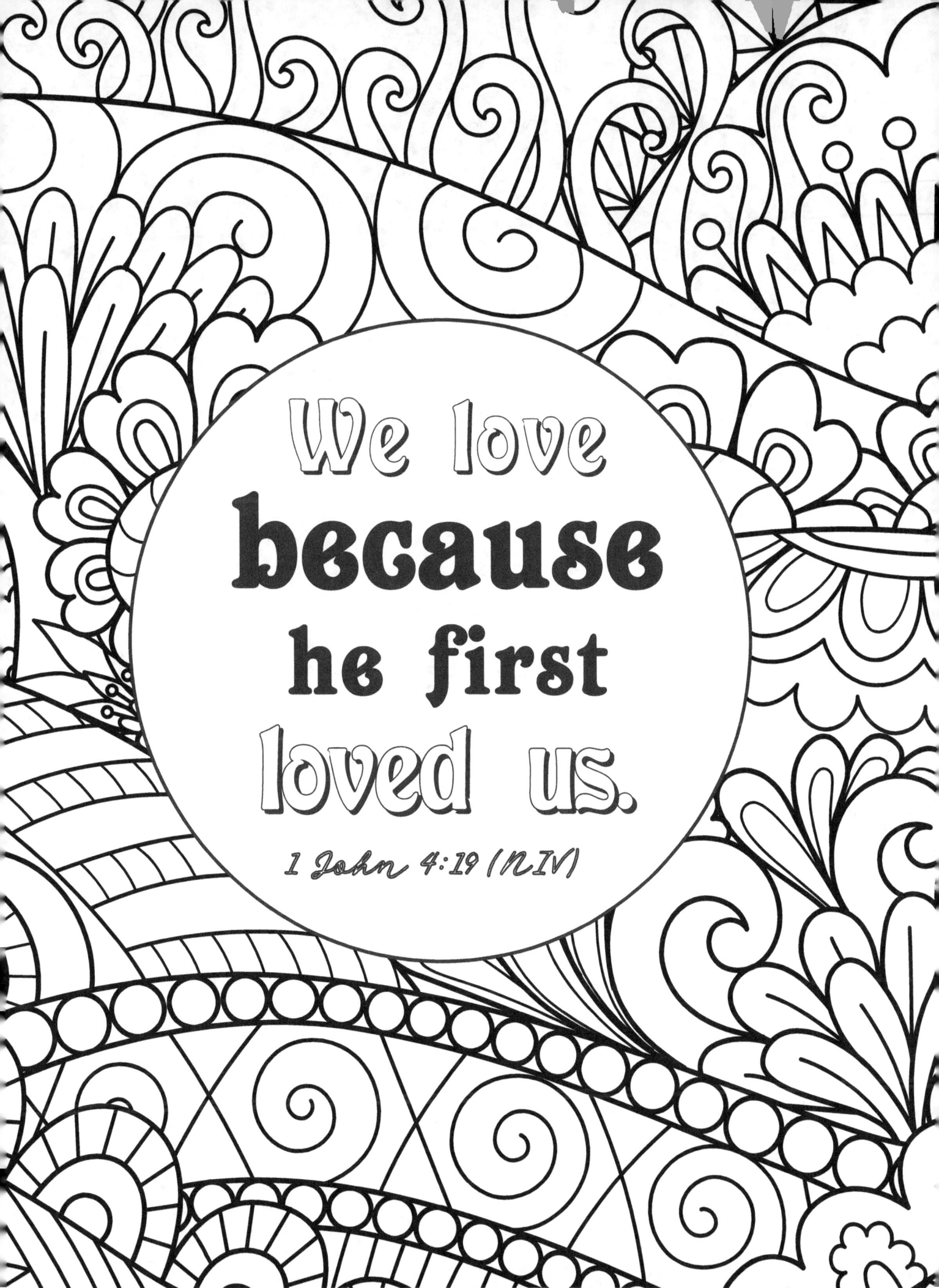

In everything he did he had great SUCCESS, Because the LORD was with him.

1 Samuel 18:14

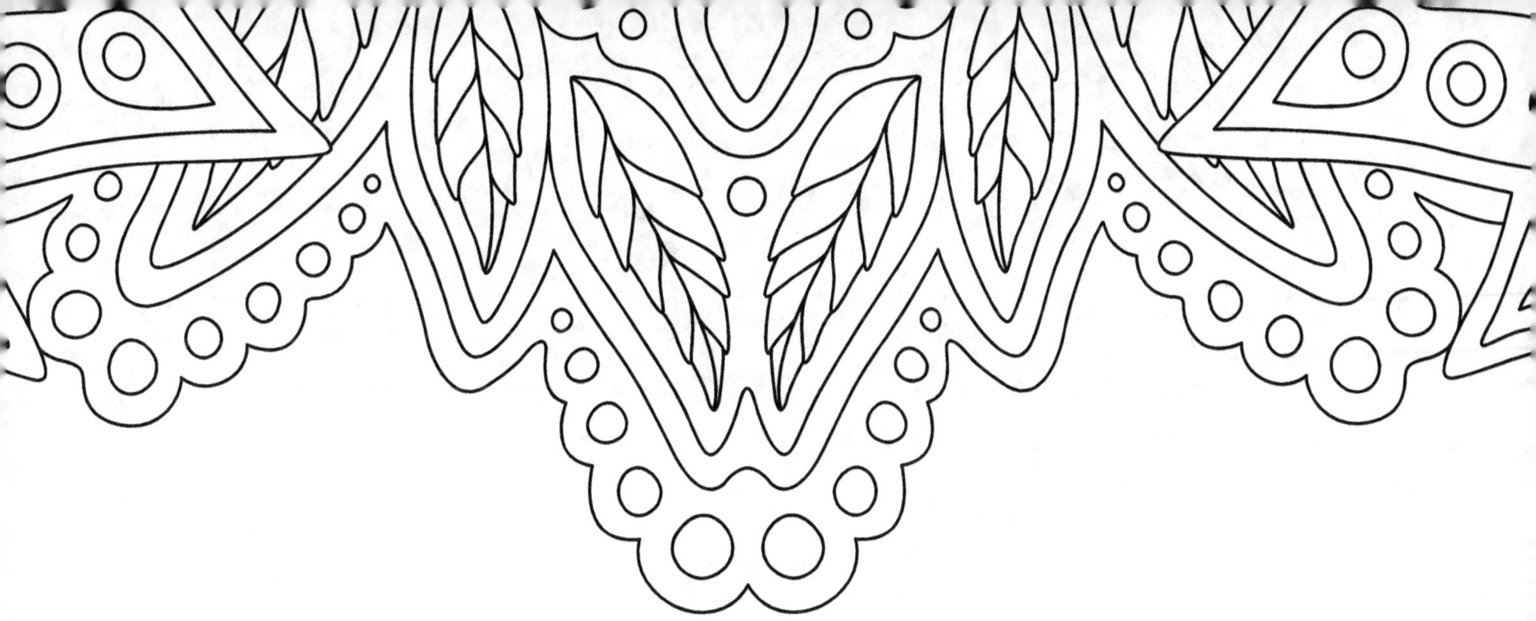

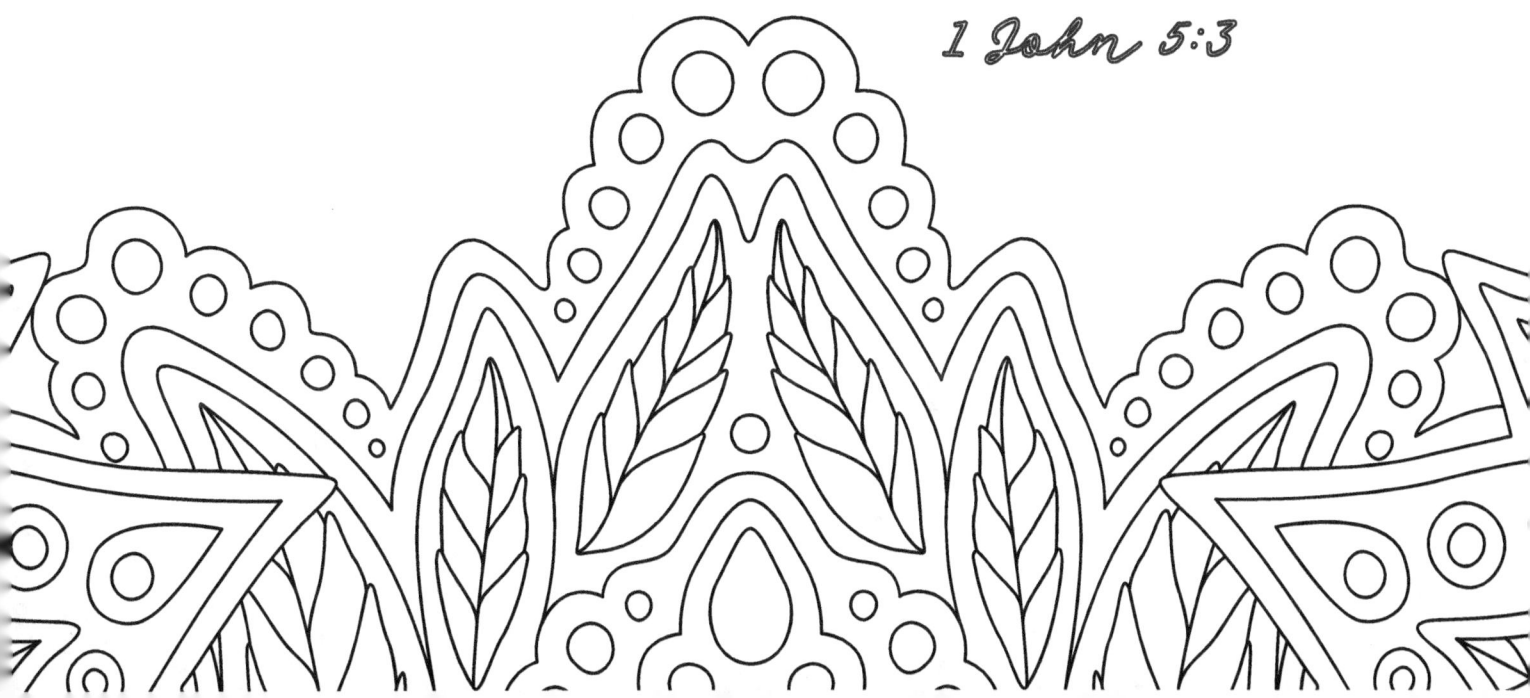

For this is the love of God, that we keep His COMMANDMENTS. And His COMMANDMENTS are not BURDENSOME.

1 John 5:3

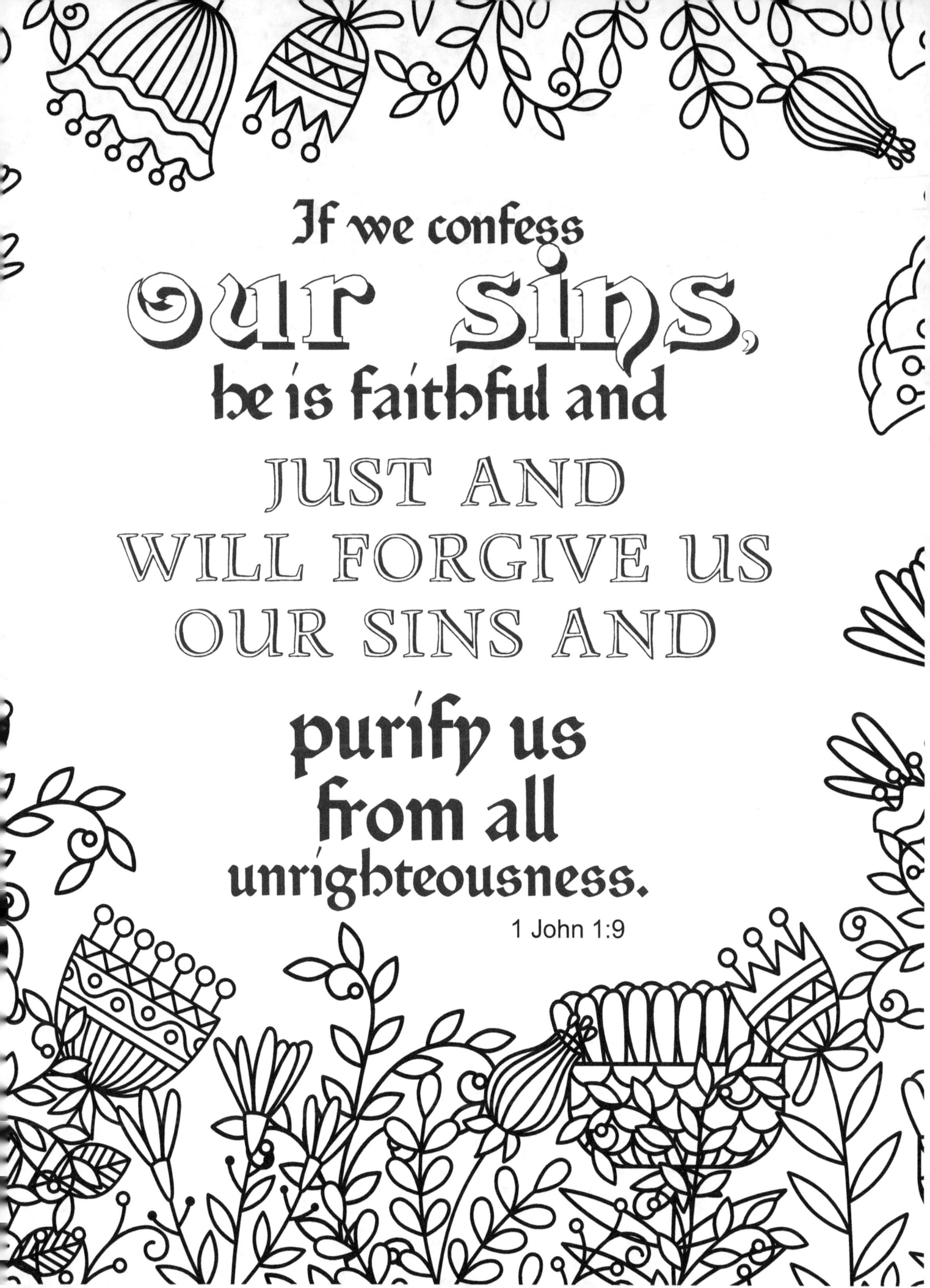

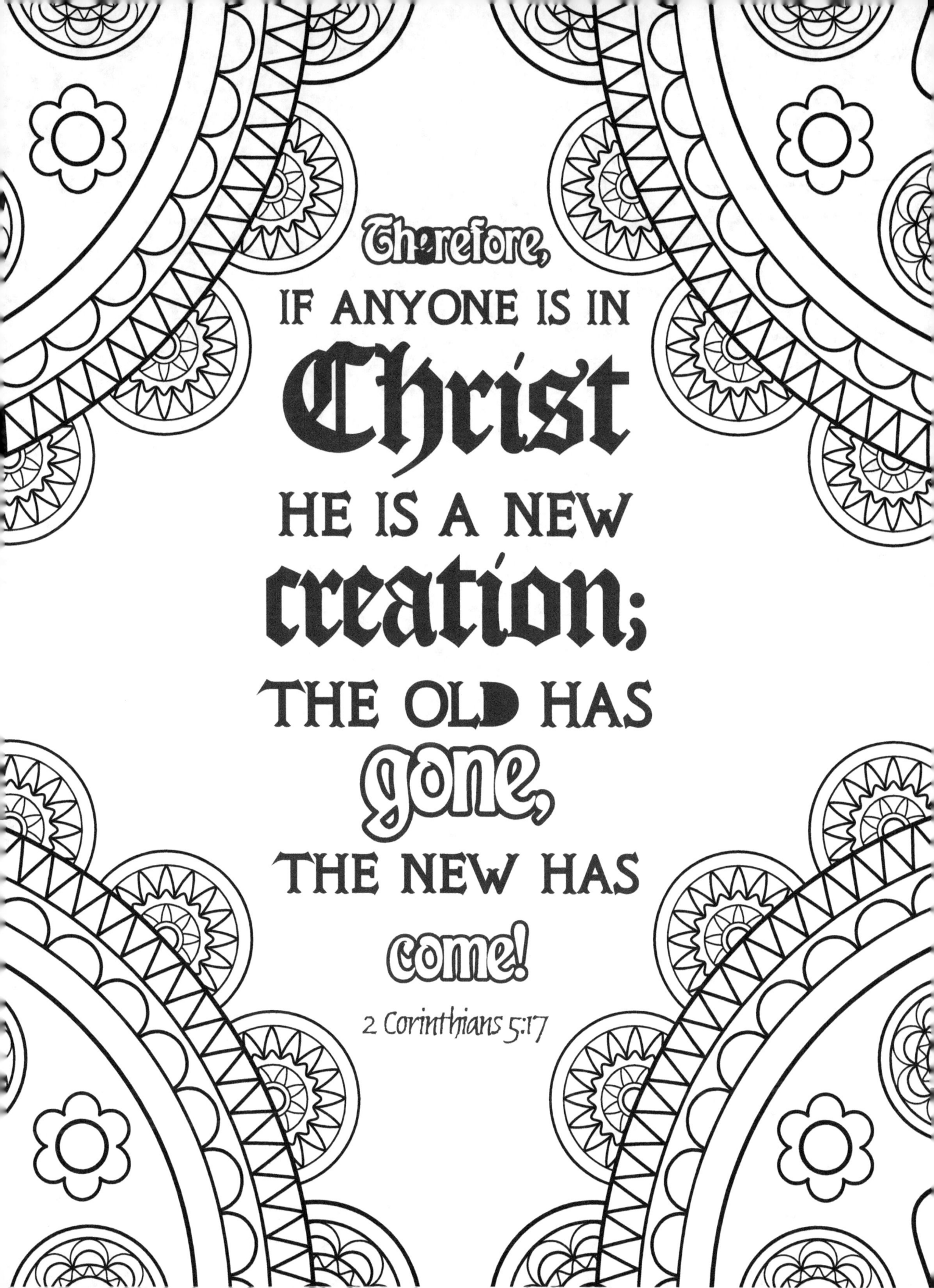

Therefore, IF ANYONE IS IN Christ HE IS A NEW creation; THE OLD HAS gone, THE NEW HAS come!

2 Corinthians 5:17

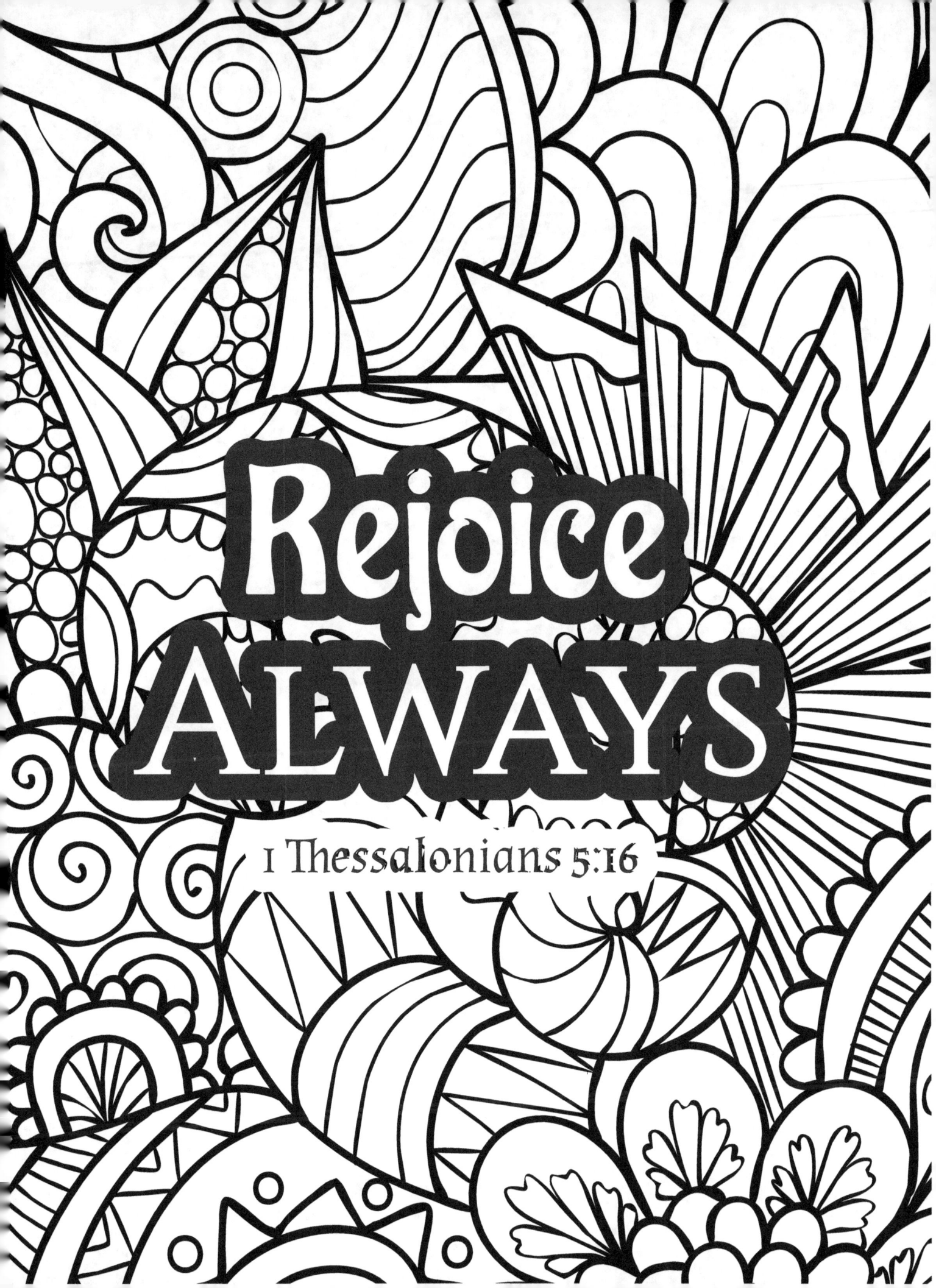

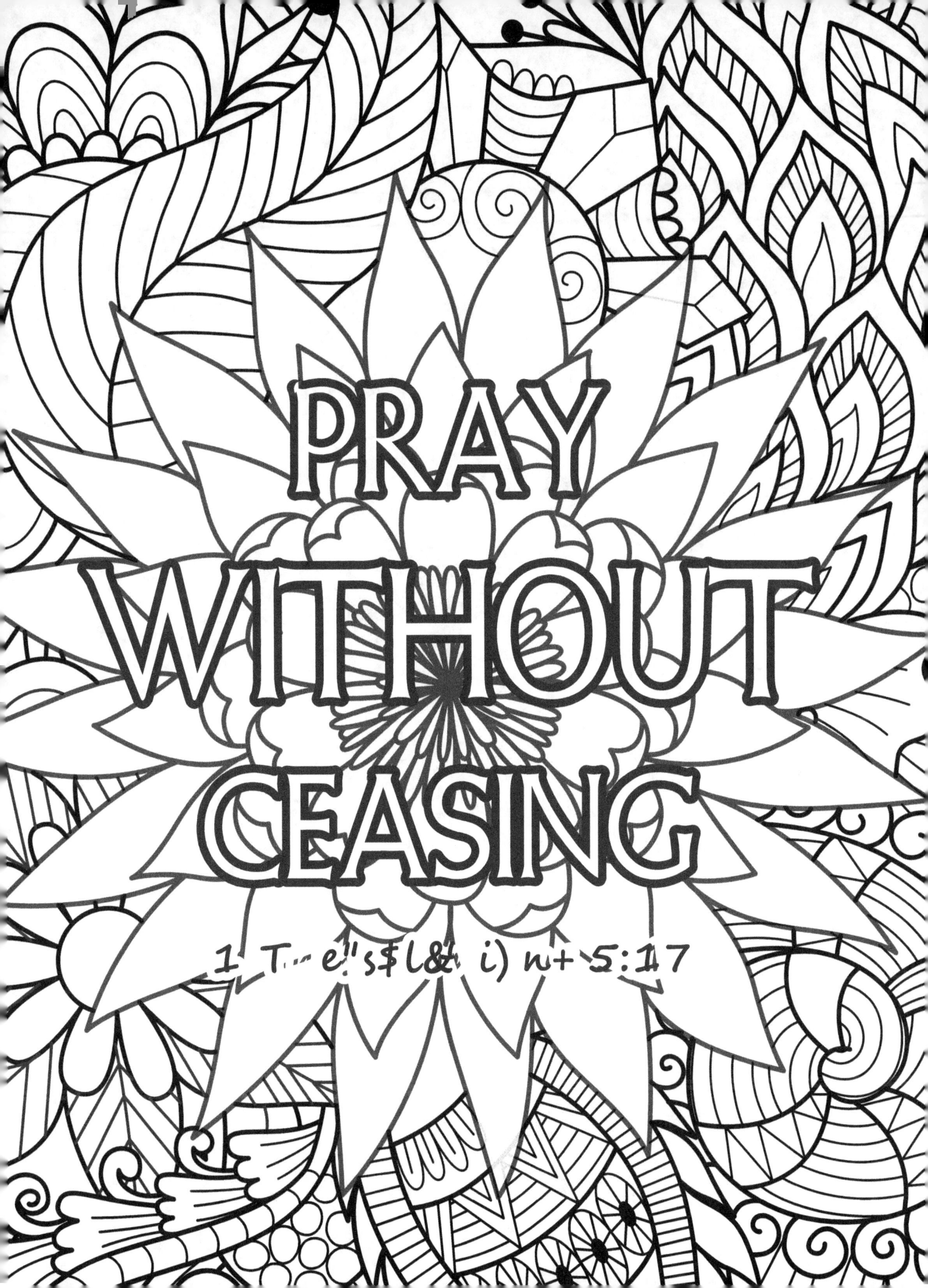

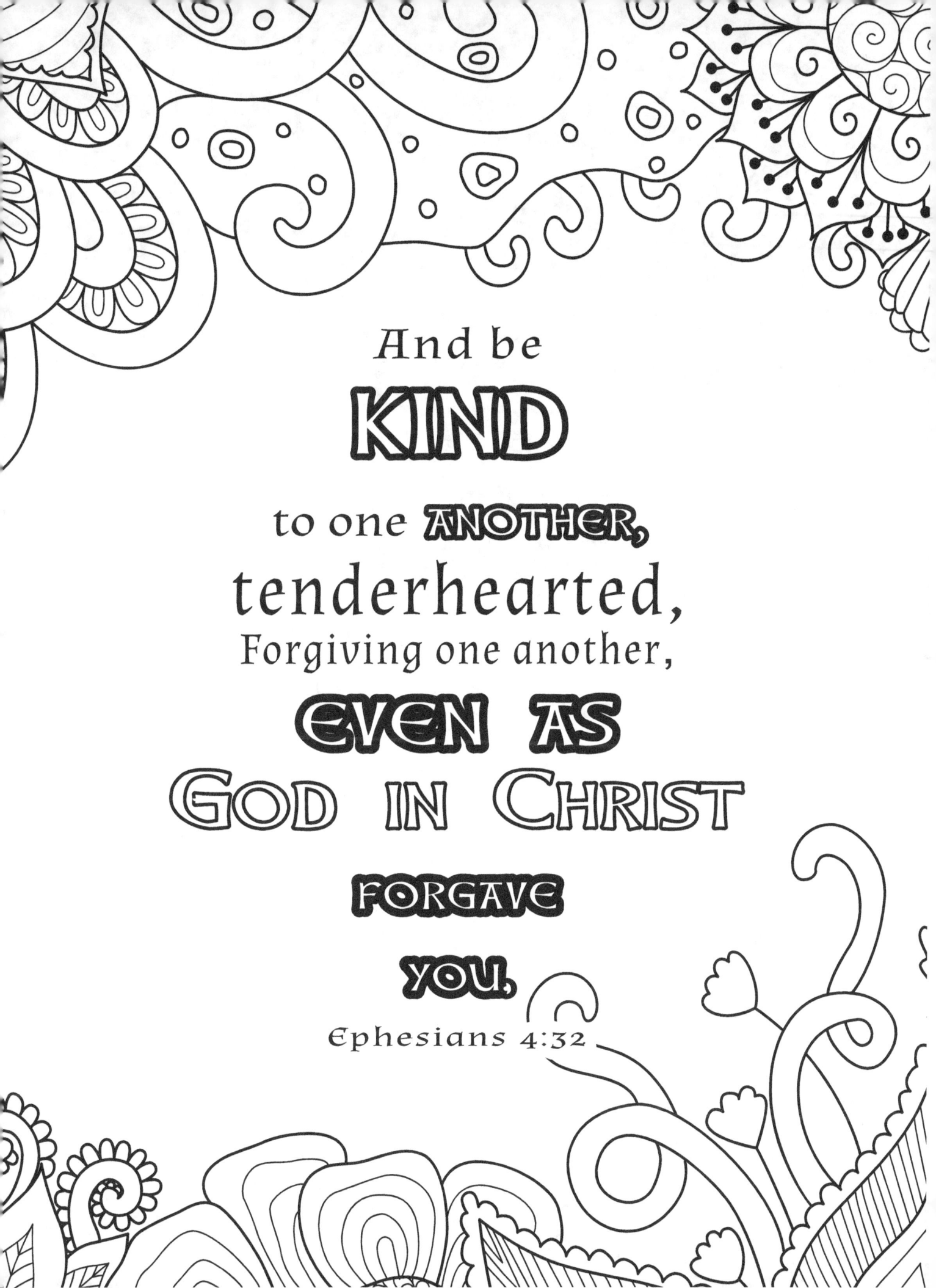

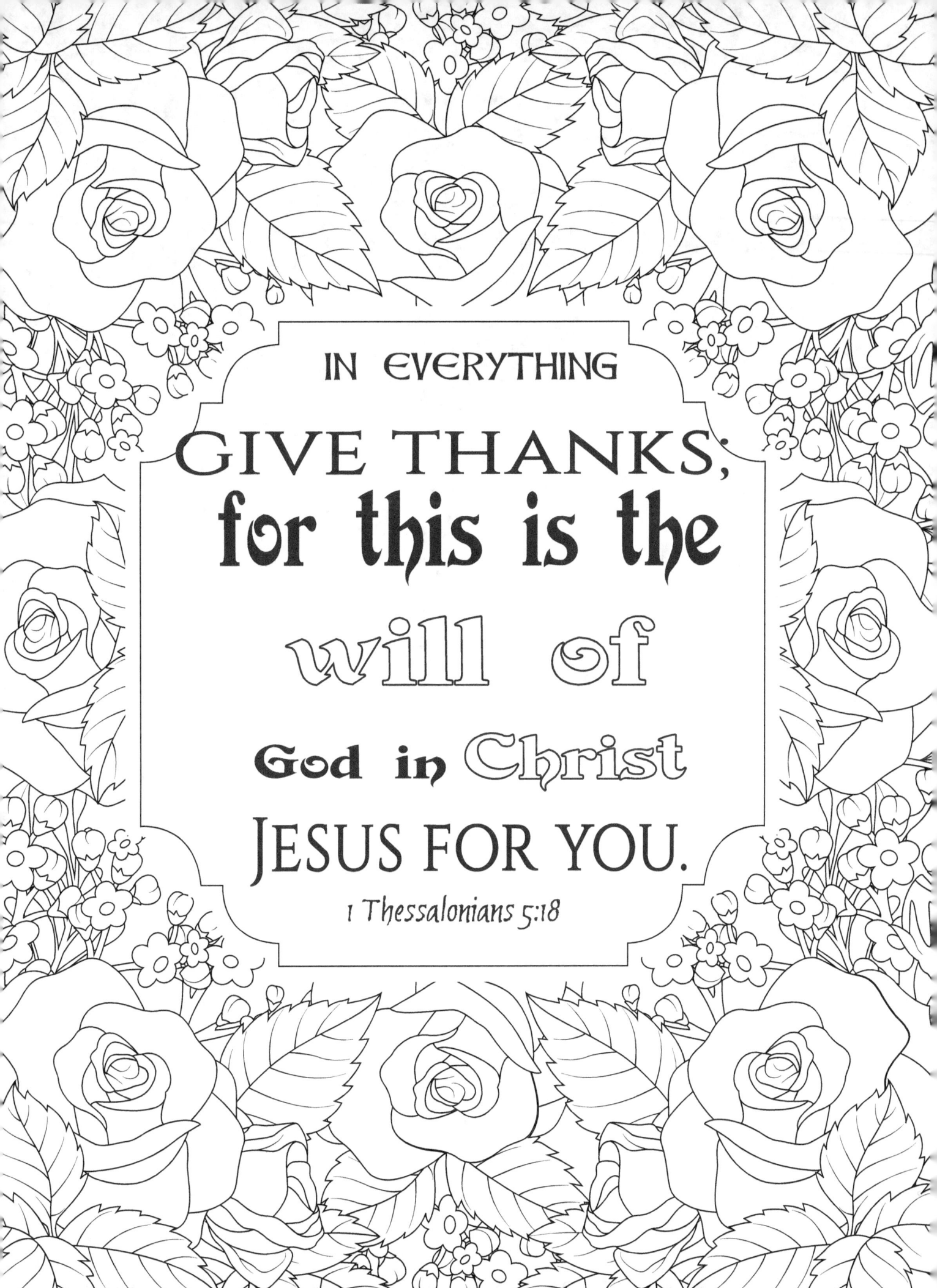

IN EVERYTHING
GIVE THANKS;
for this is the
will of
God in Christ
JESUS FOR YOU.
1 Thessalonians 5:18

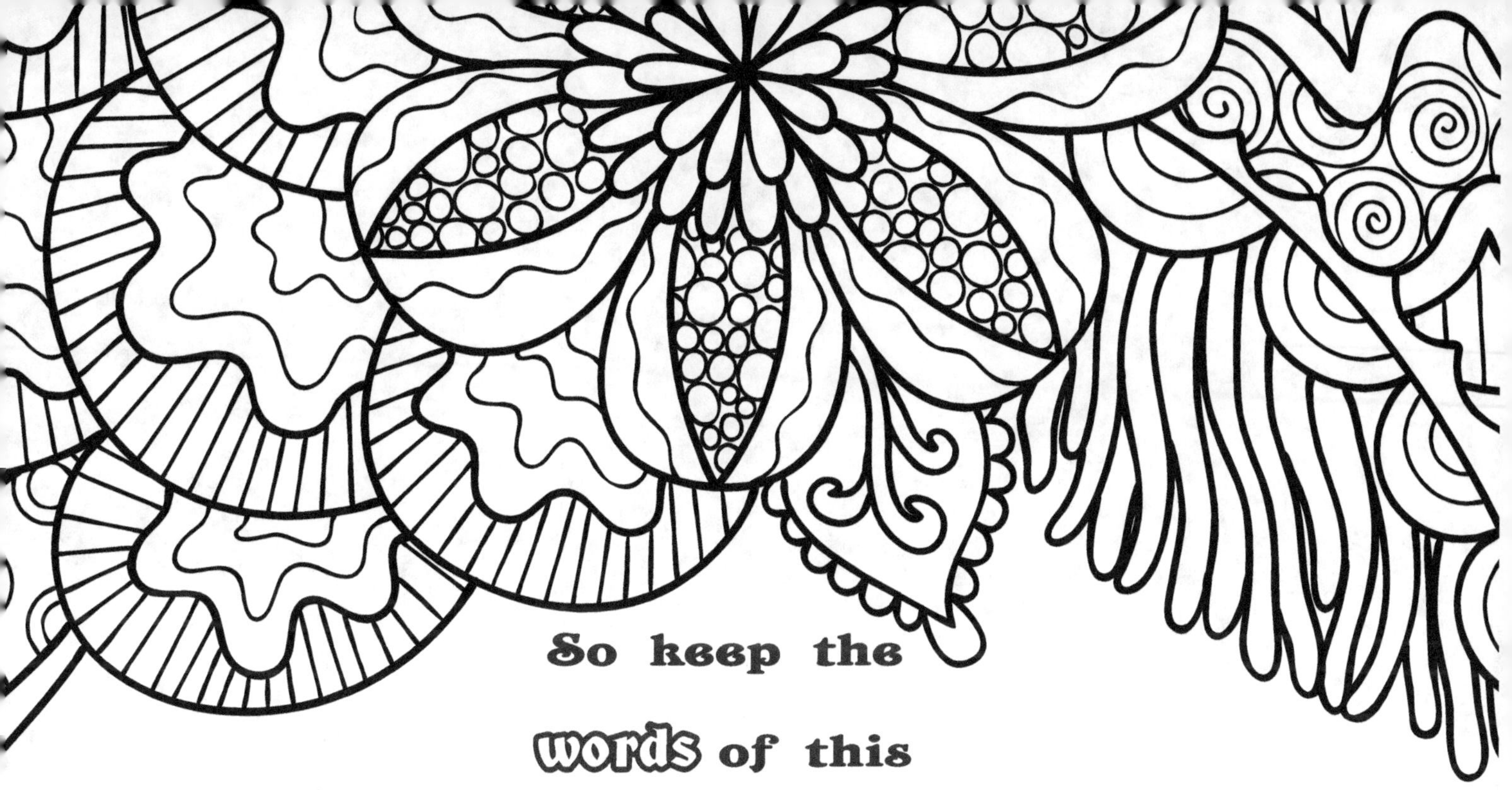

So keep the

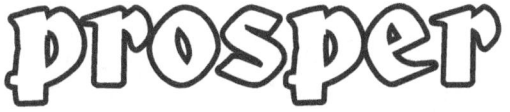words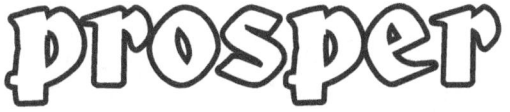 of this

covenant

to do them, that you may

prosper

in all that

you do.

Deuteronomy 29:9

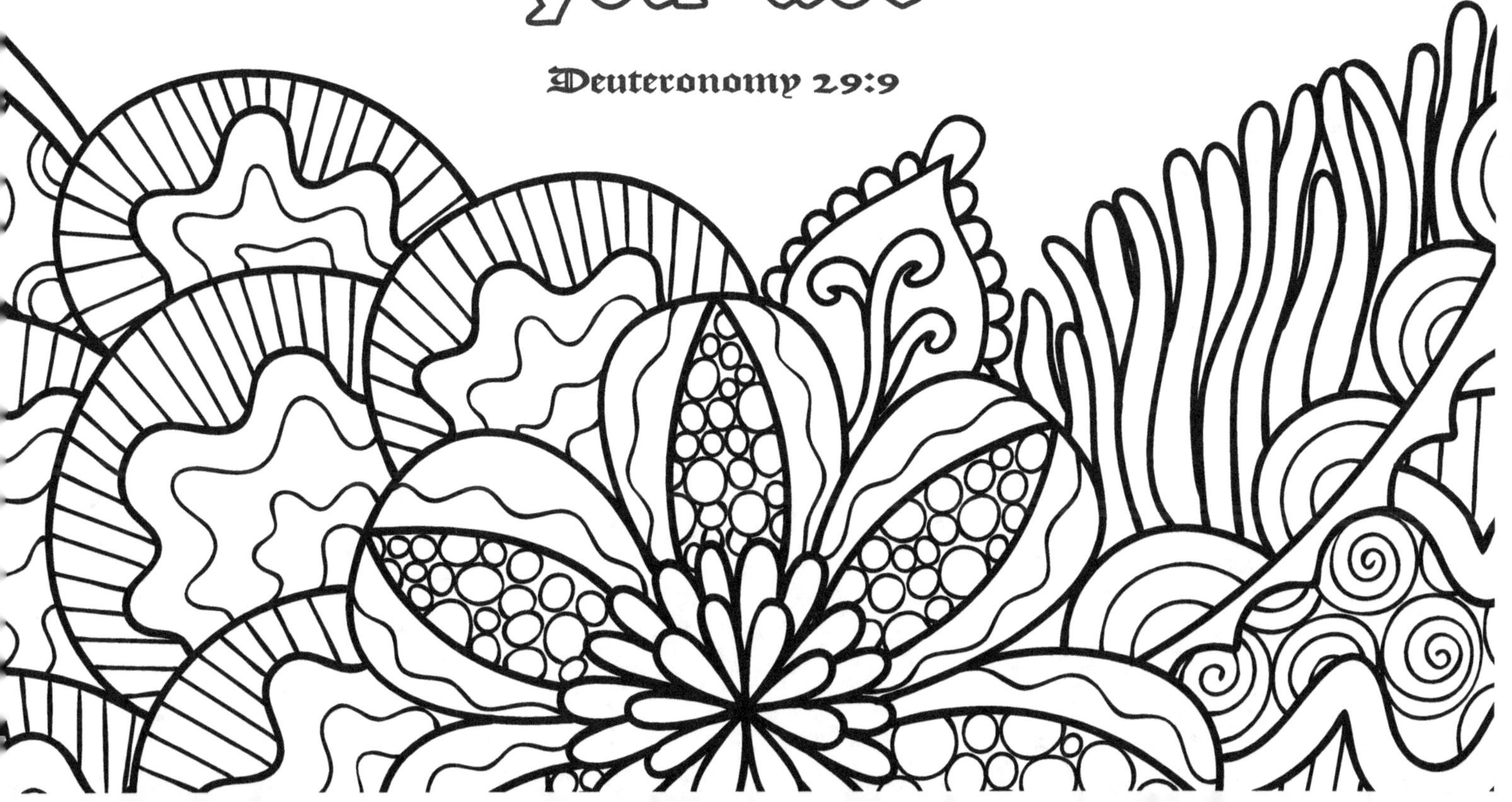

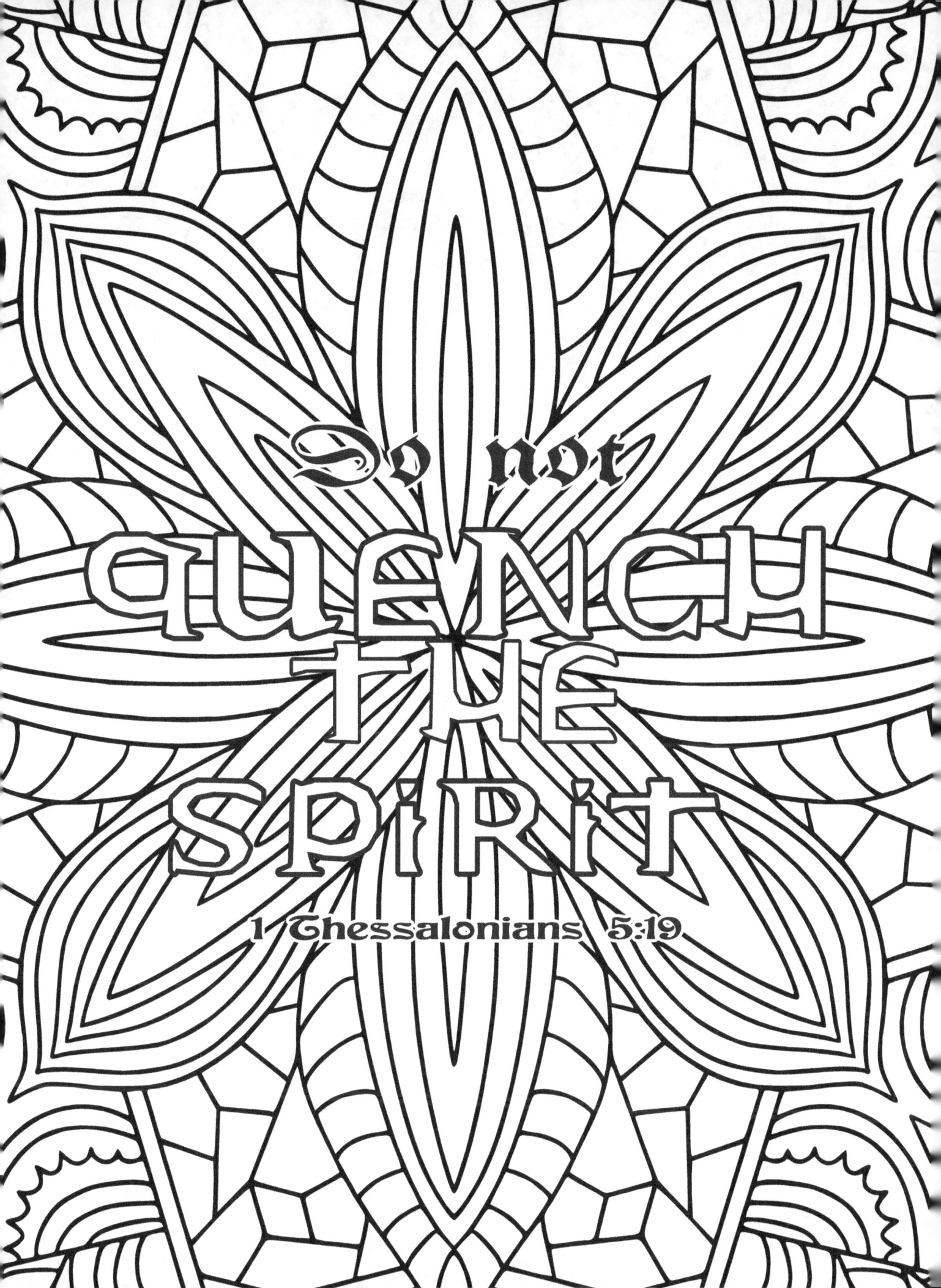

Do not QUENCH THE SPIRIT

1 Thessalonians 5:19

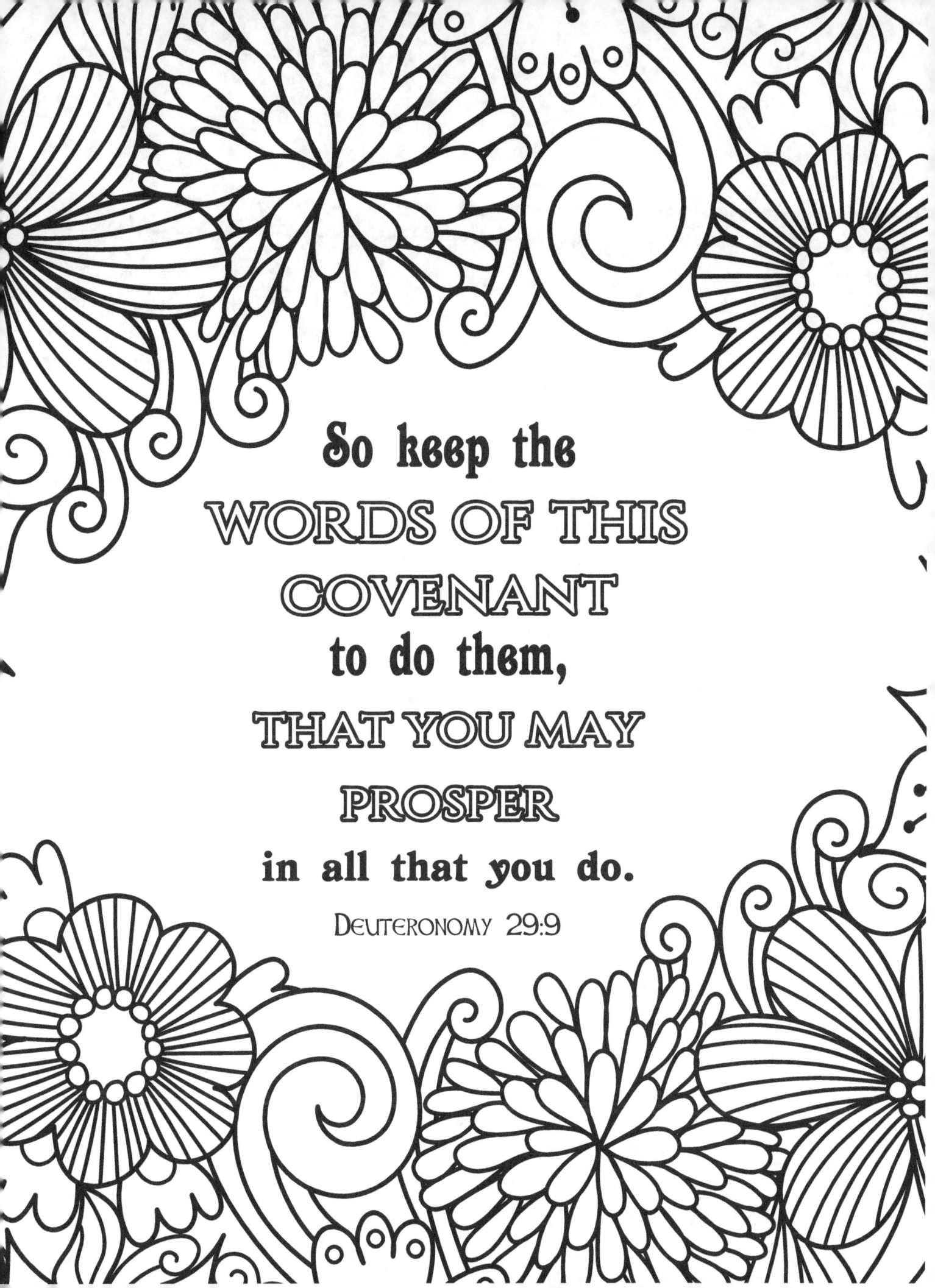

So keep the
WORDS OF THIS
COVENANT
to do them,
THAT YOU MAY
PROSPER
in all that you do.

Deuteronomy 29:9

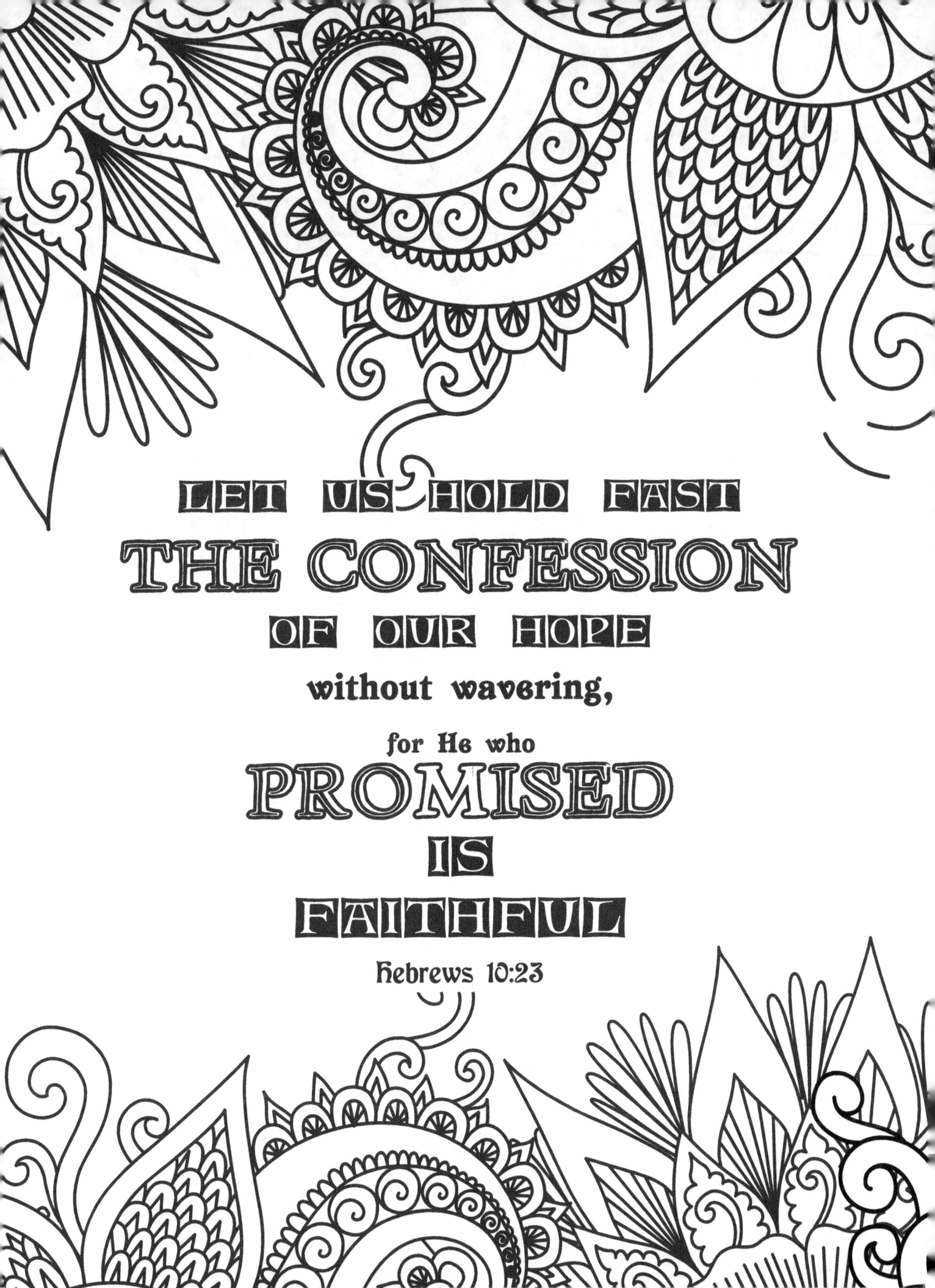

LET US HOLD FAST
THE CONFESSION
OF OUR HOPE
without wavering,
for He who
PROMISED
IS
FAITHFUL
Hebrews 10:23

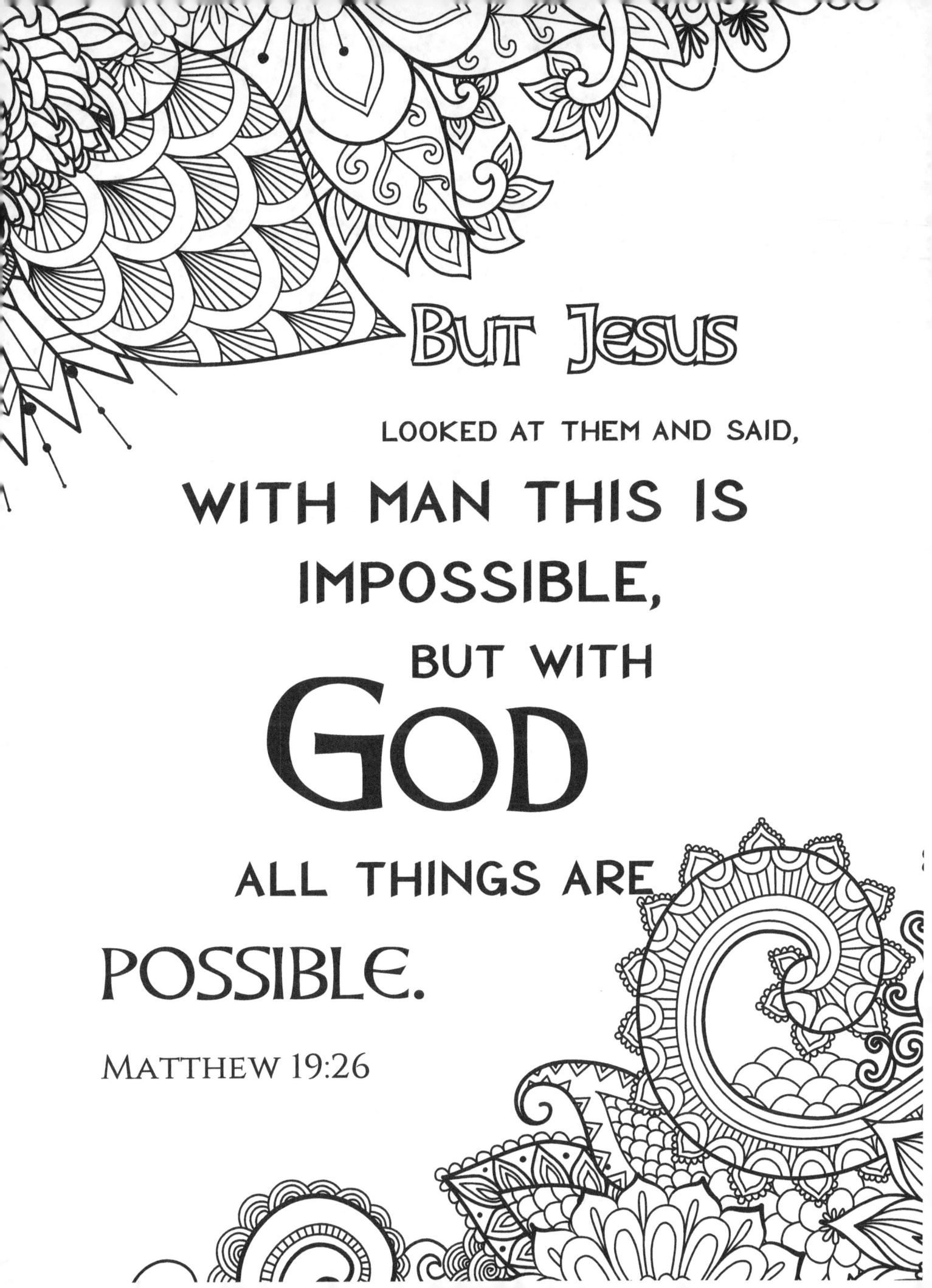

But Jesus

LOOKED AT THEM AND SAID,

WITH MAN THIS IS

IMPOSSIBLE,

BUT WITH

GOD

ALL THINGS ARE

POSSIBLE.

MATTHEW 19:26

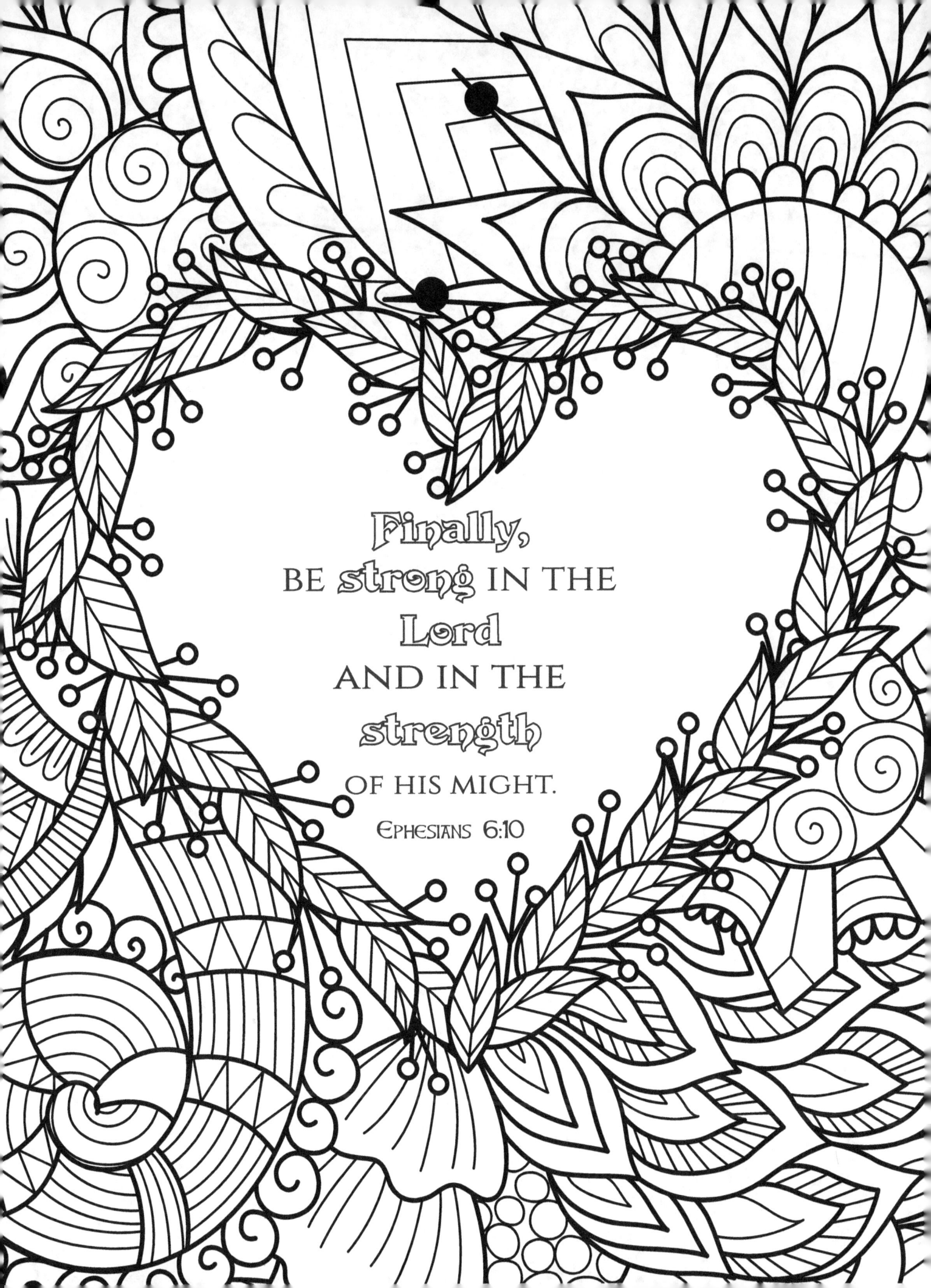

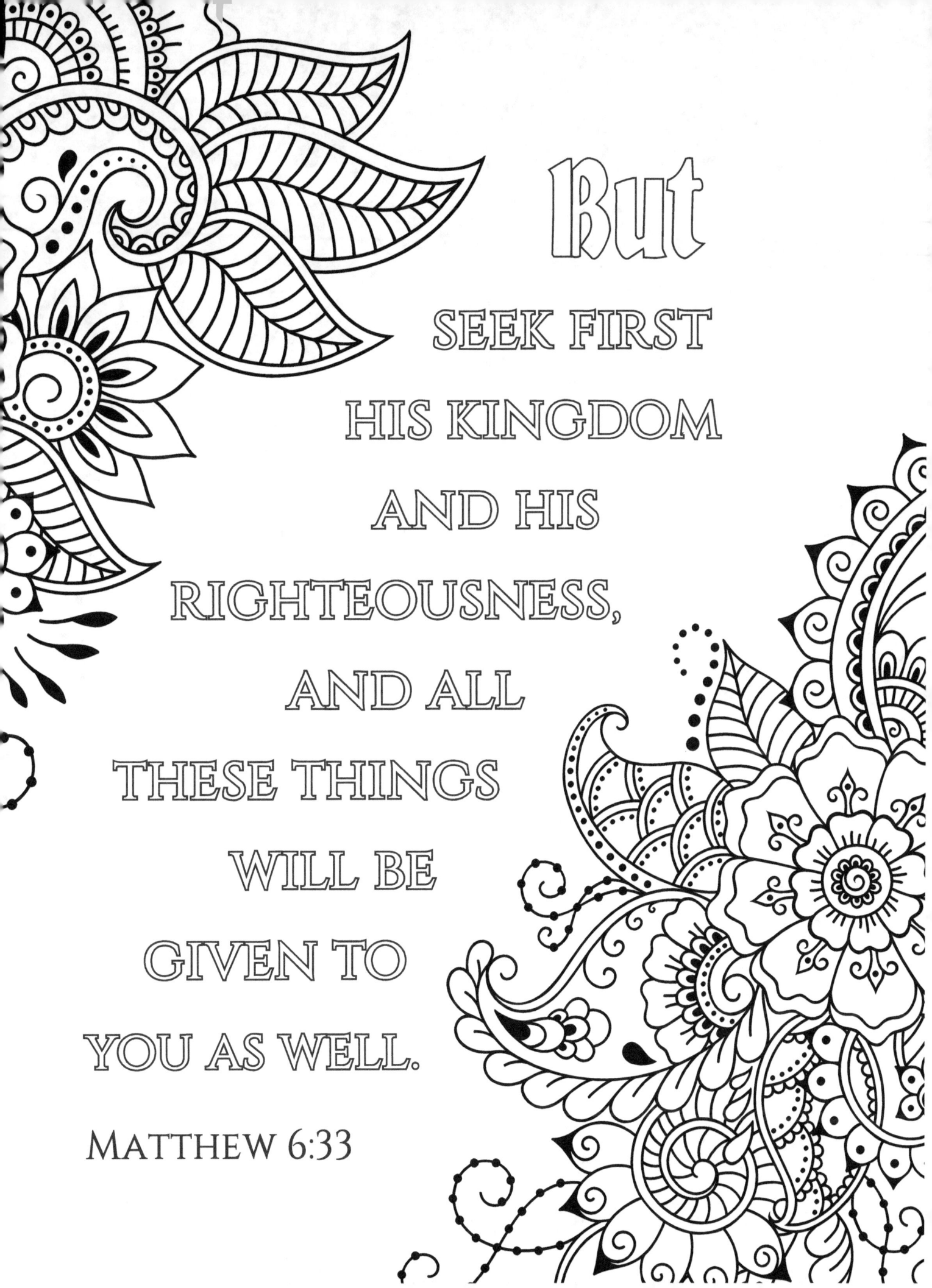

But
SEEK FIRST
HIS KINGDOM
AND HIS
RIGHTEOUSNESS,
AND ALL
THESE THINGS
WILL BE
GIVEN TO
YOU AS WELL.

MATTHEW 6:33

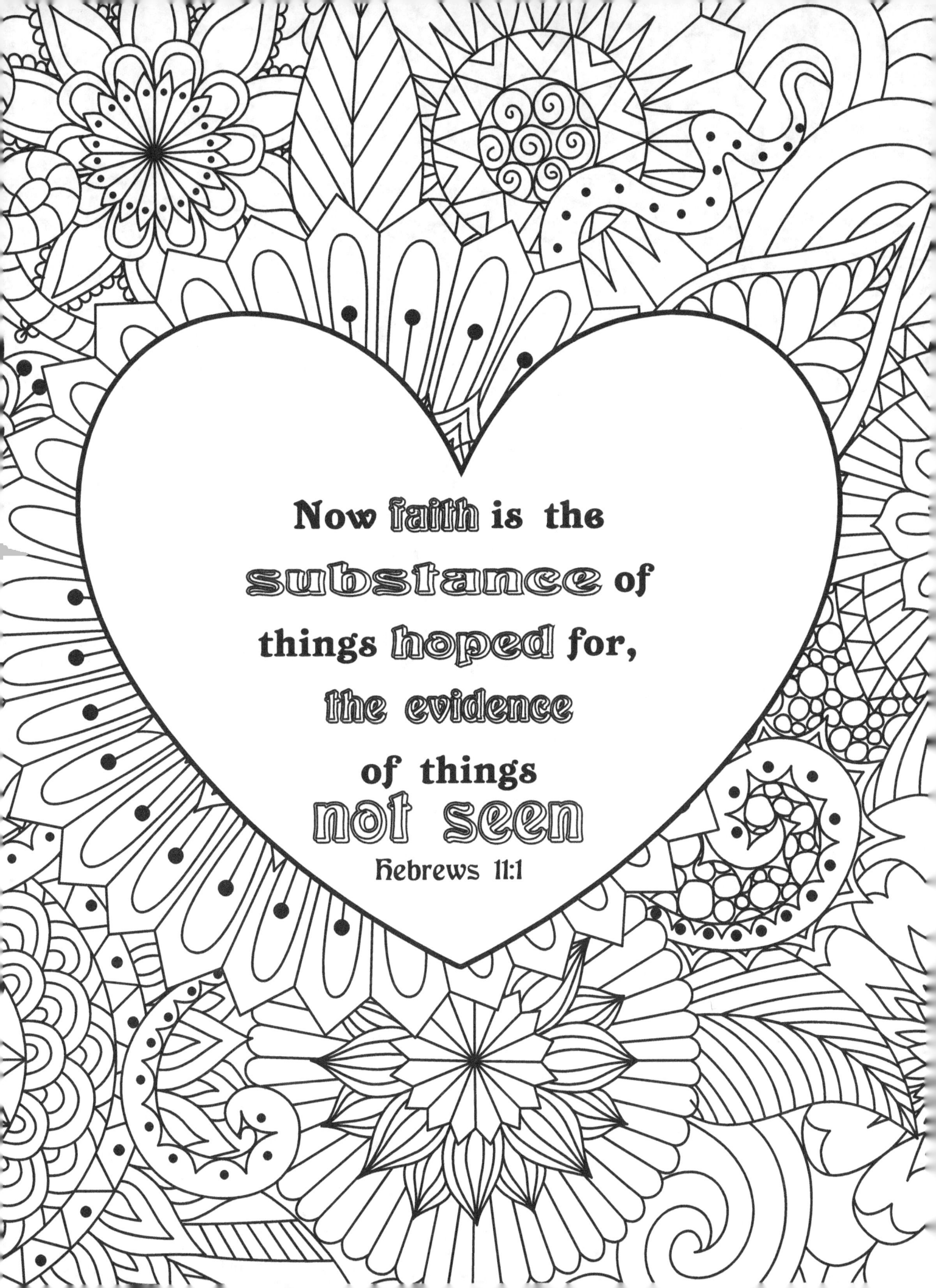

Now faith is the substance of things hoped for, the evidence of things not seen

Hebrews 11:1

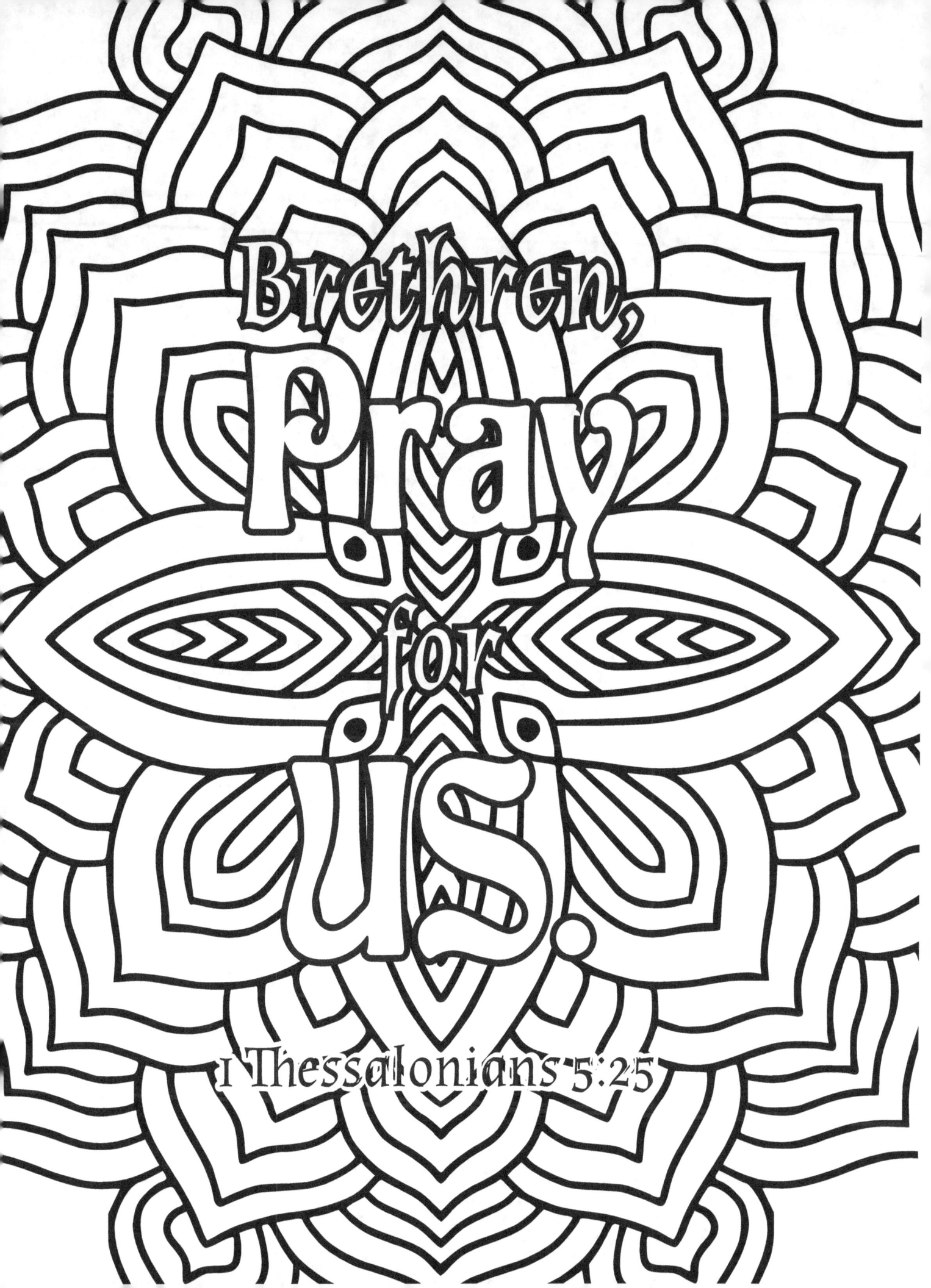

Brethren, Pray for us.

1 Thessalonians 5:25

Without counsel, plans go awry, But in the multitude of counselors they are established.

Proverbs 15:22

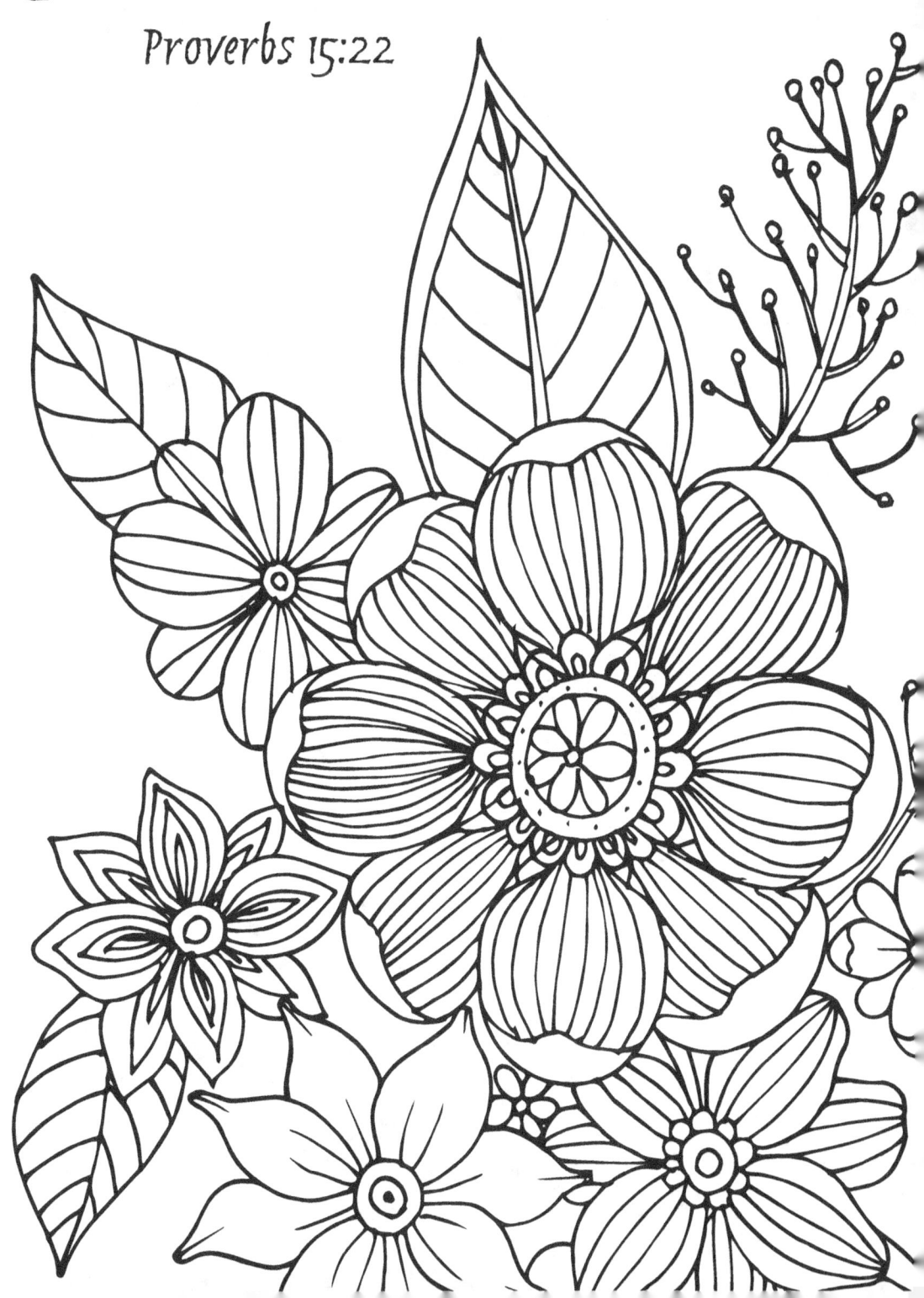

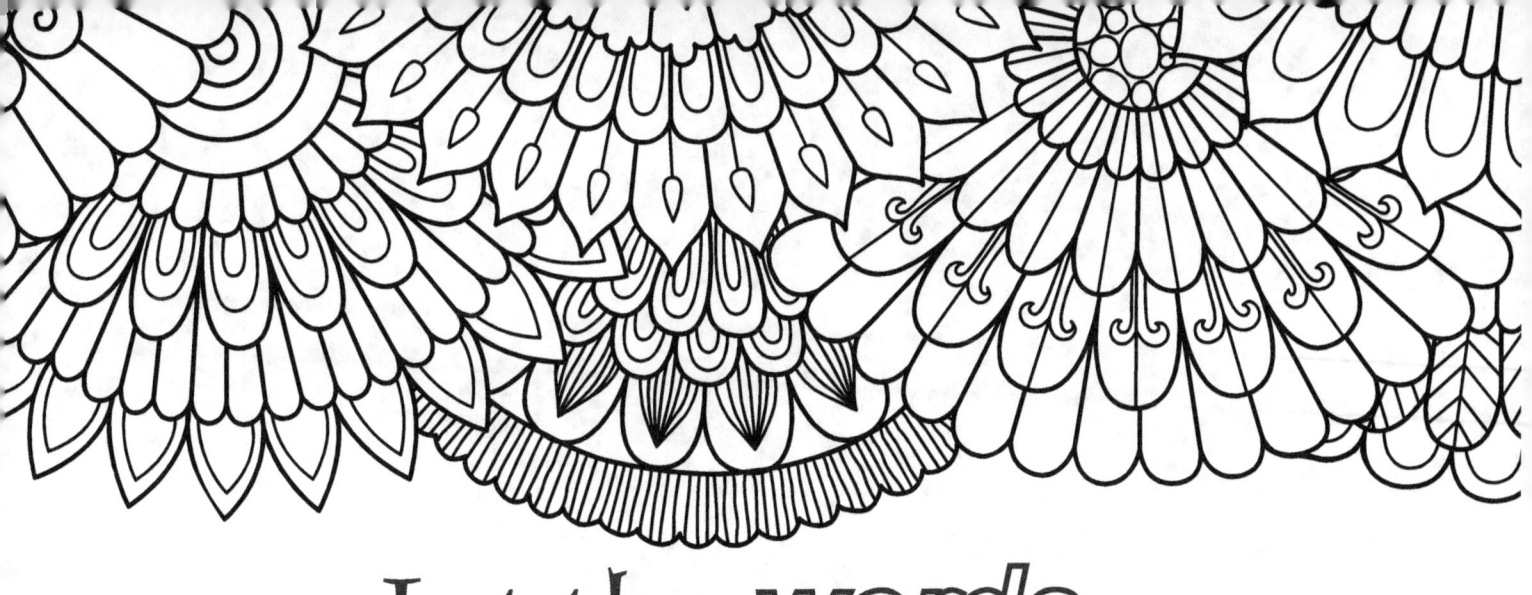

Let the *words*
of my mouth
and the *meditation*
of my heart
Be *acceptable*
in **Your Sight**

Psalm 19:14

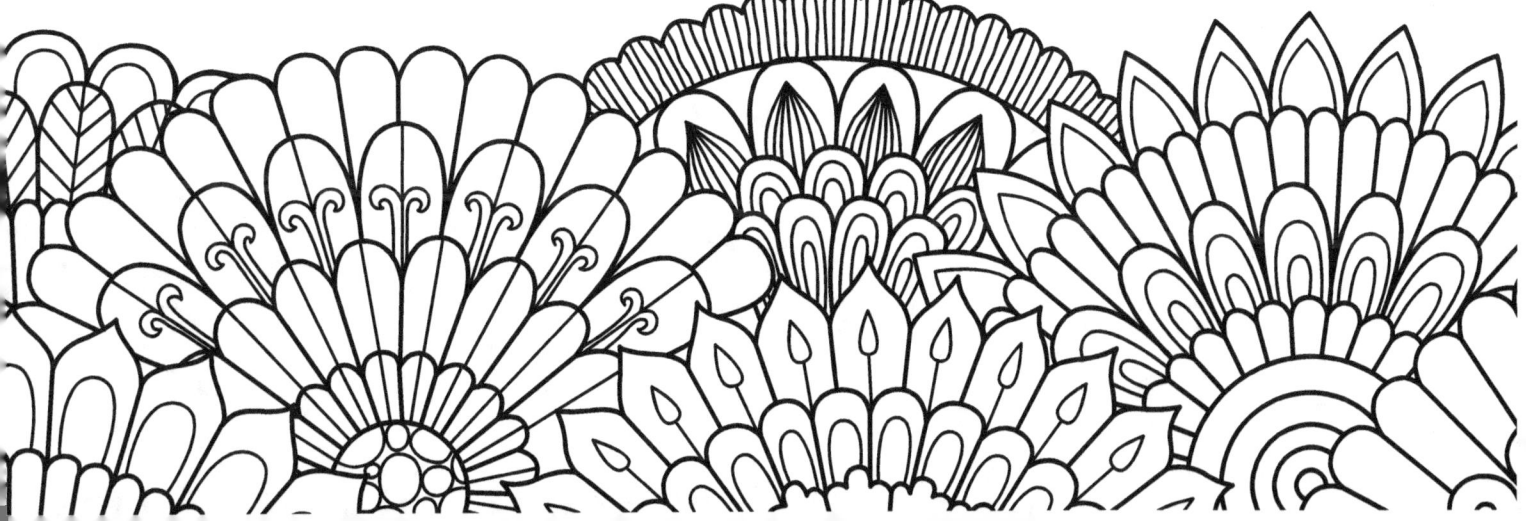

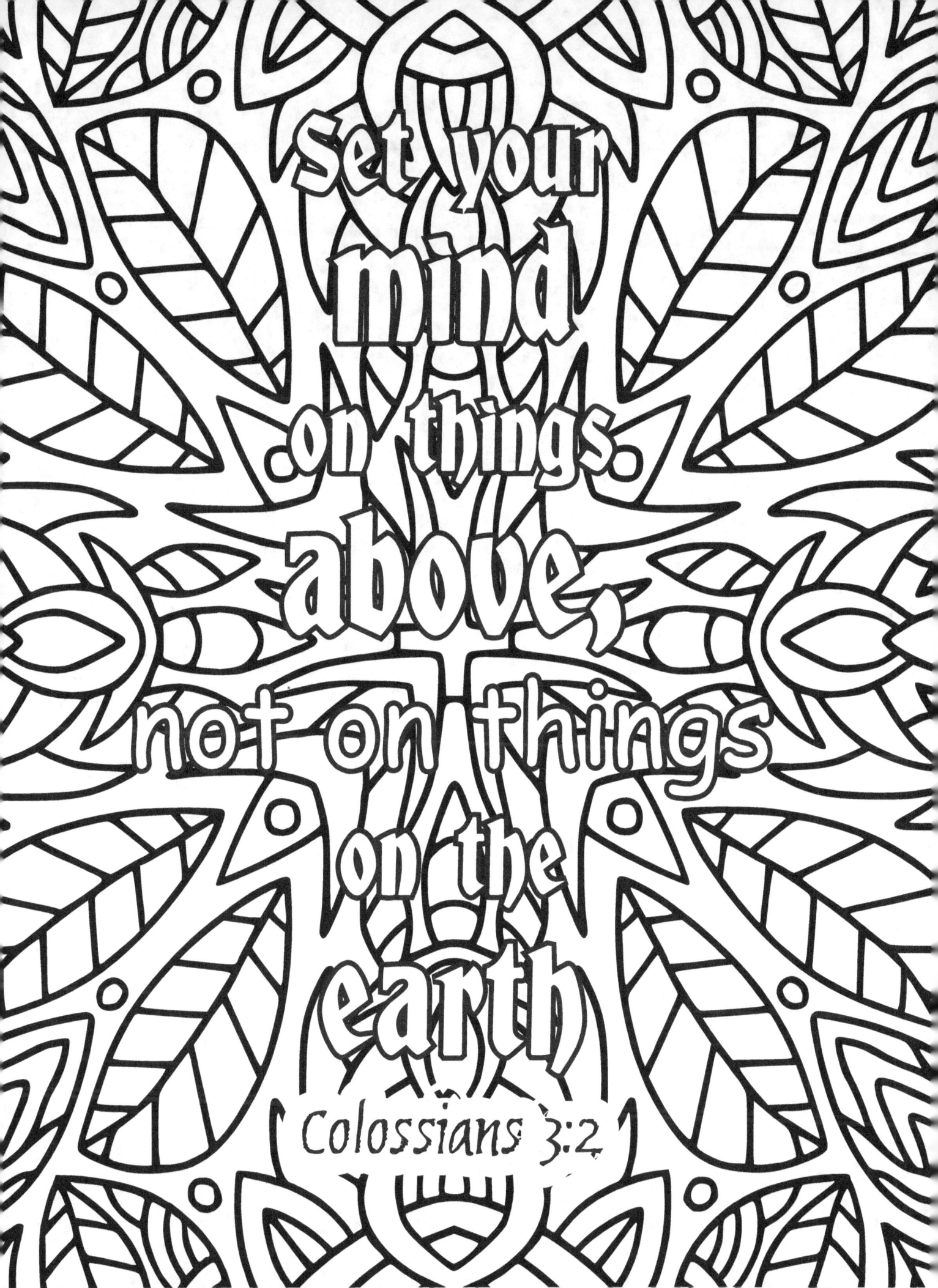

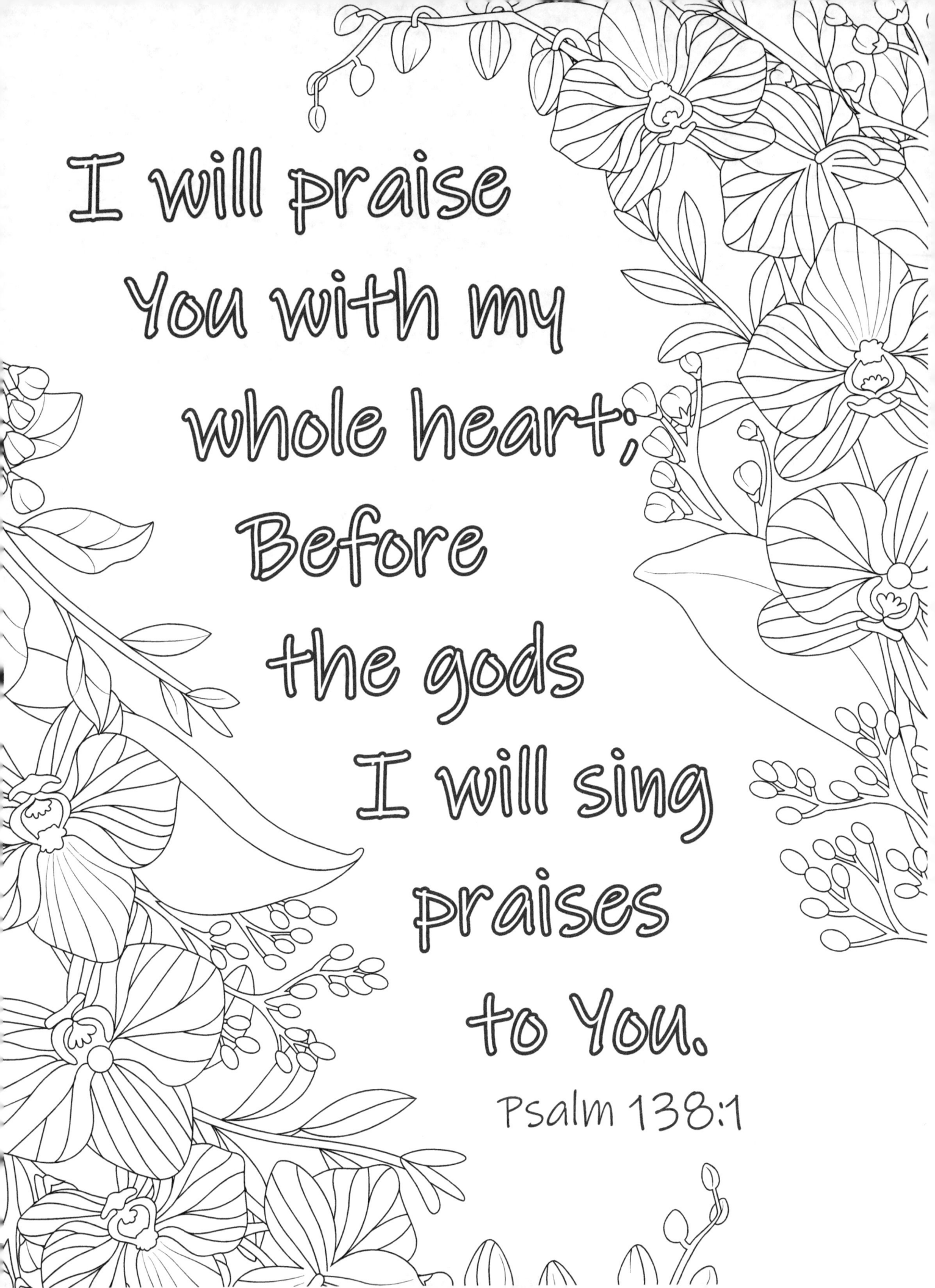

I will praise You with my whole heart; Before the gods I will sing praises to You.

Psalm 138:1

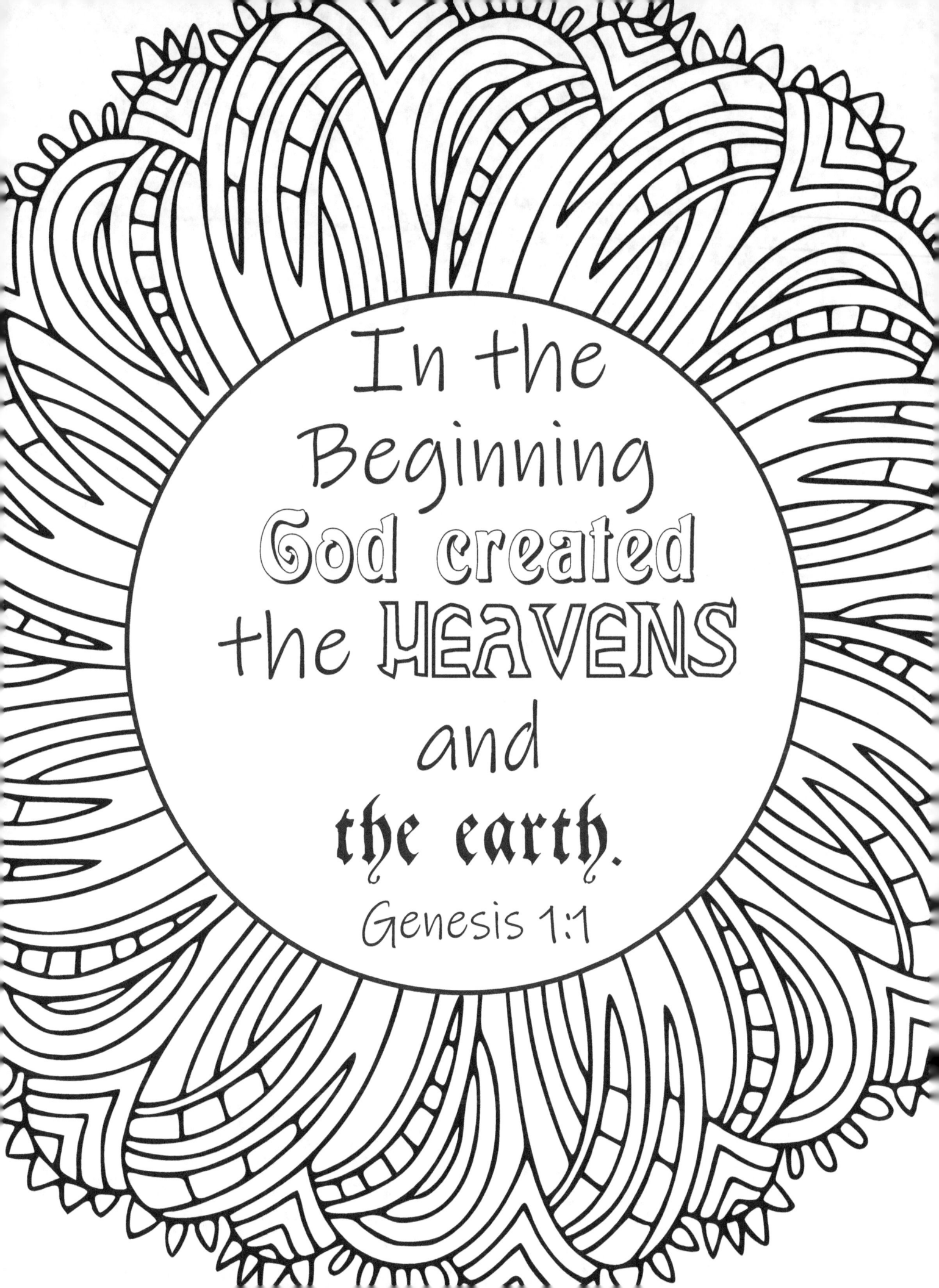

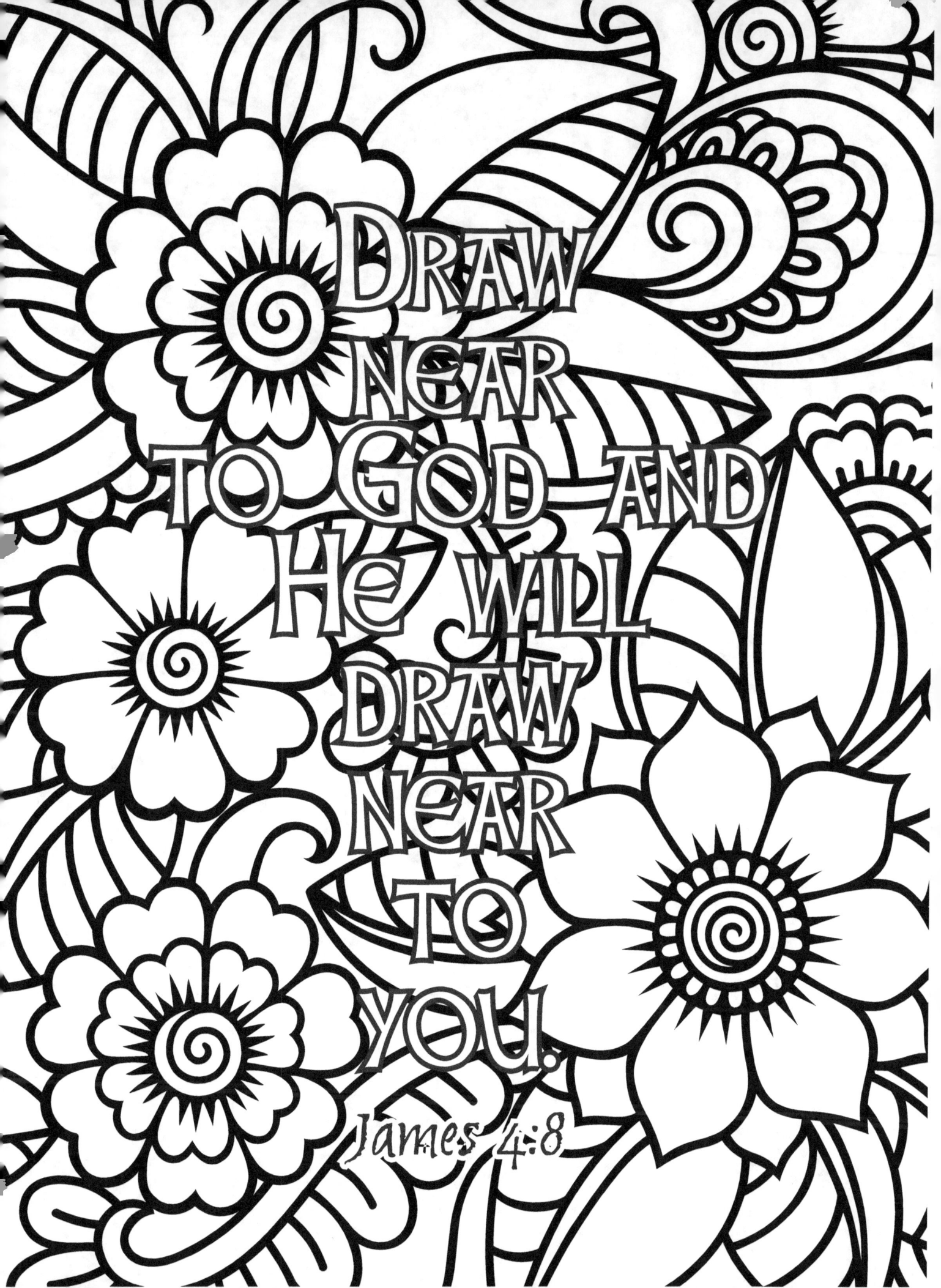

Delight yourself also in the Lord, And He shall give you the desires of your heart.

Psalm 37:4

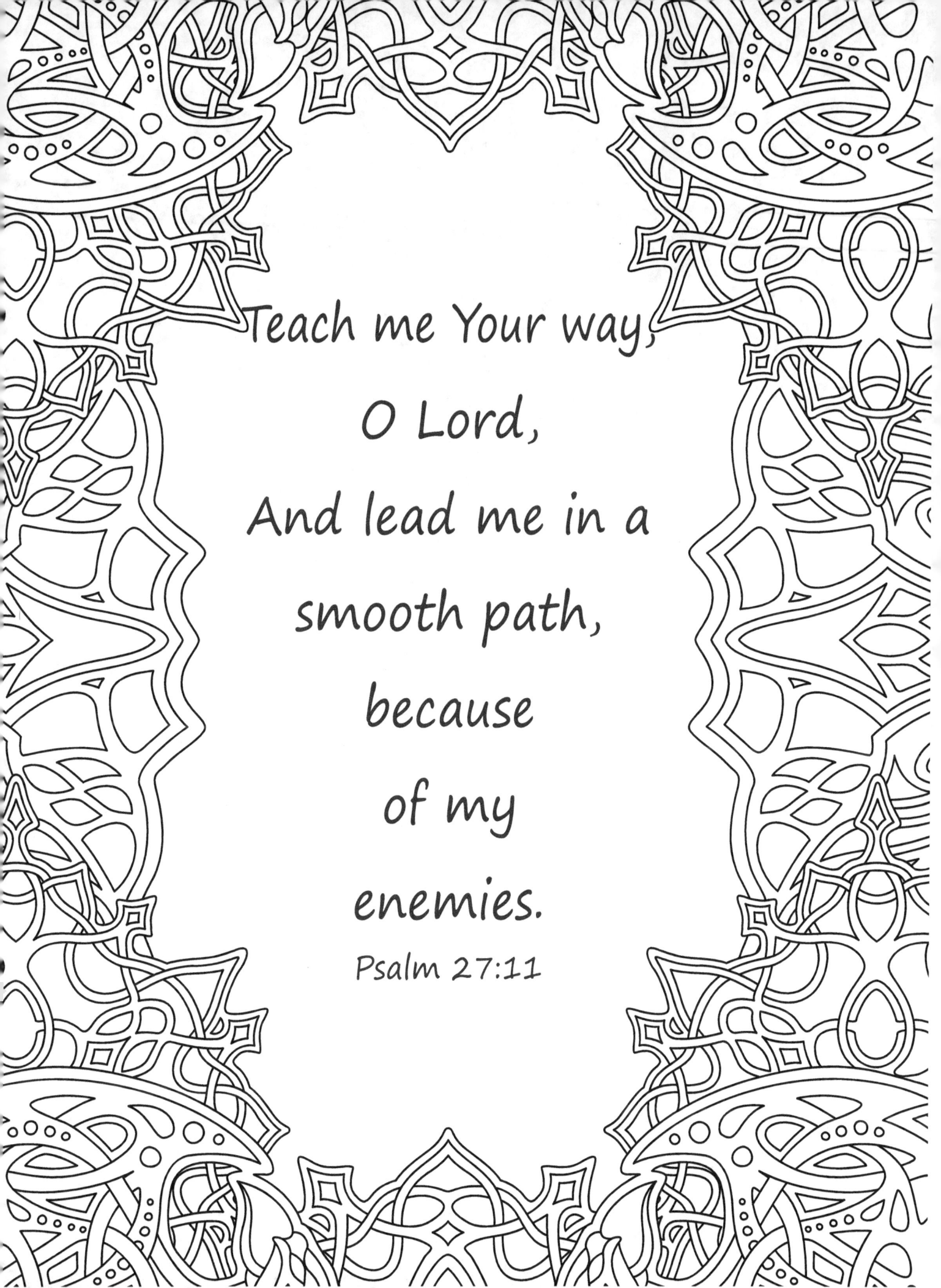

Teach me Your way,
O Lord,
And lead me in a
smooth path,
because
of my
enemies.
Psalm 27:11

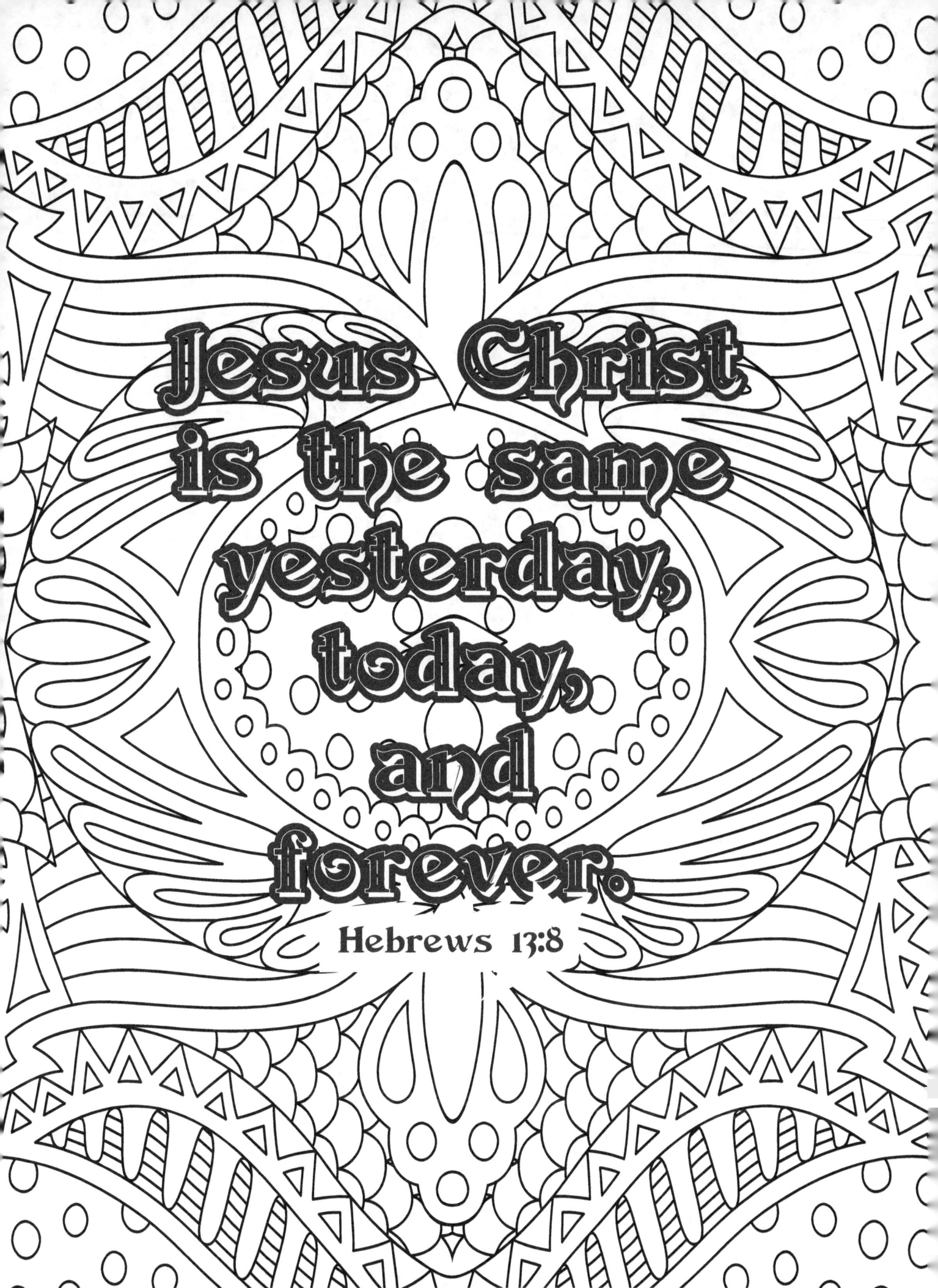

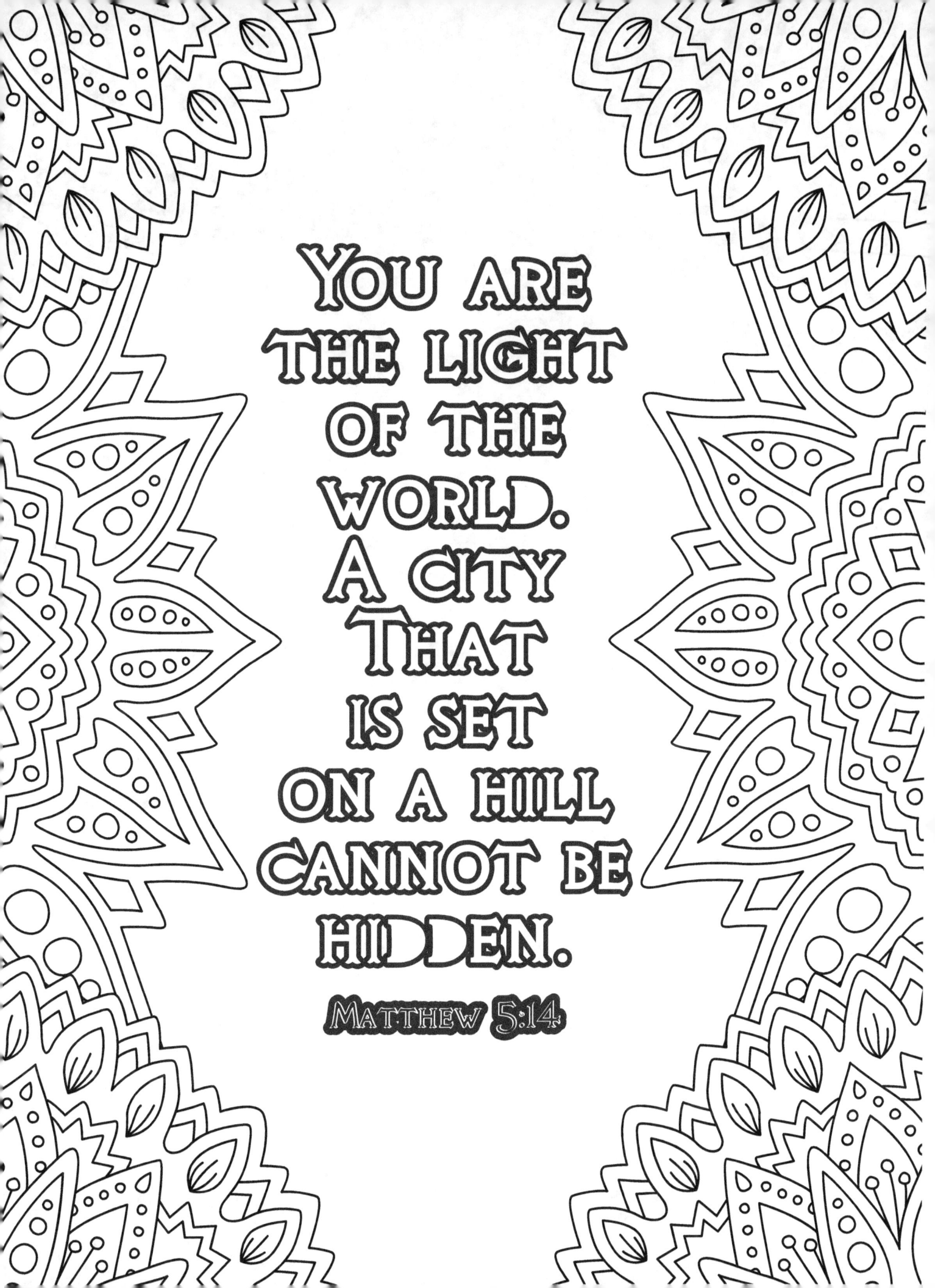

You are the light of the world. A city that is set on a hill cannot be hidden.

Matthew 5:14

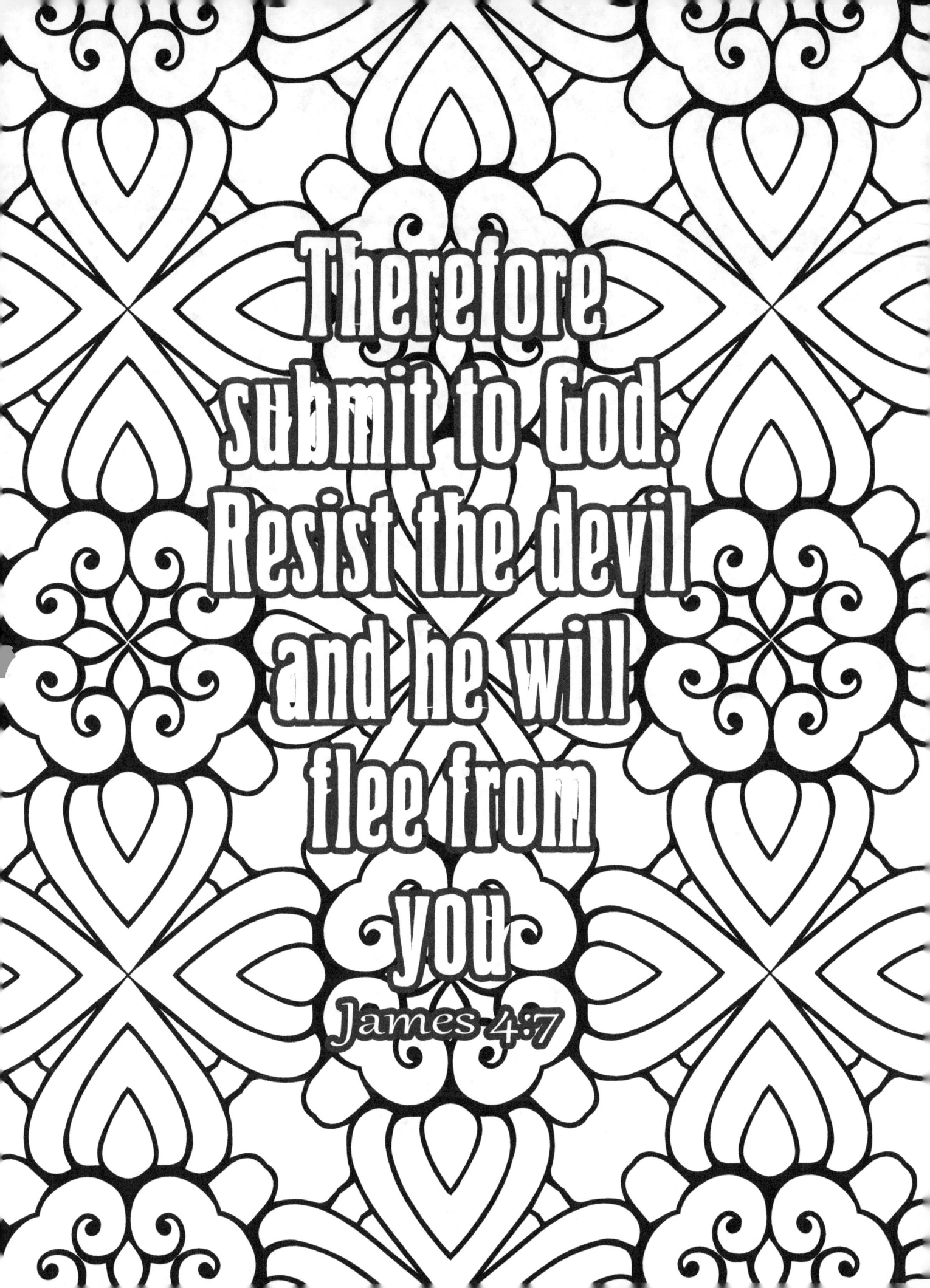

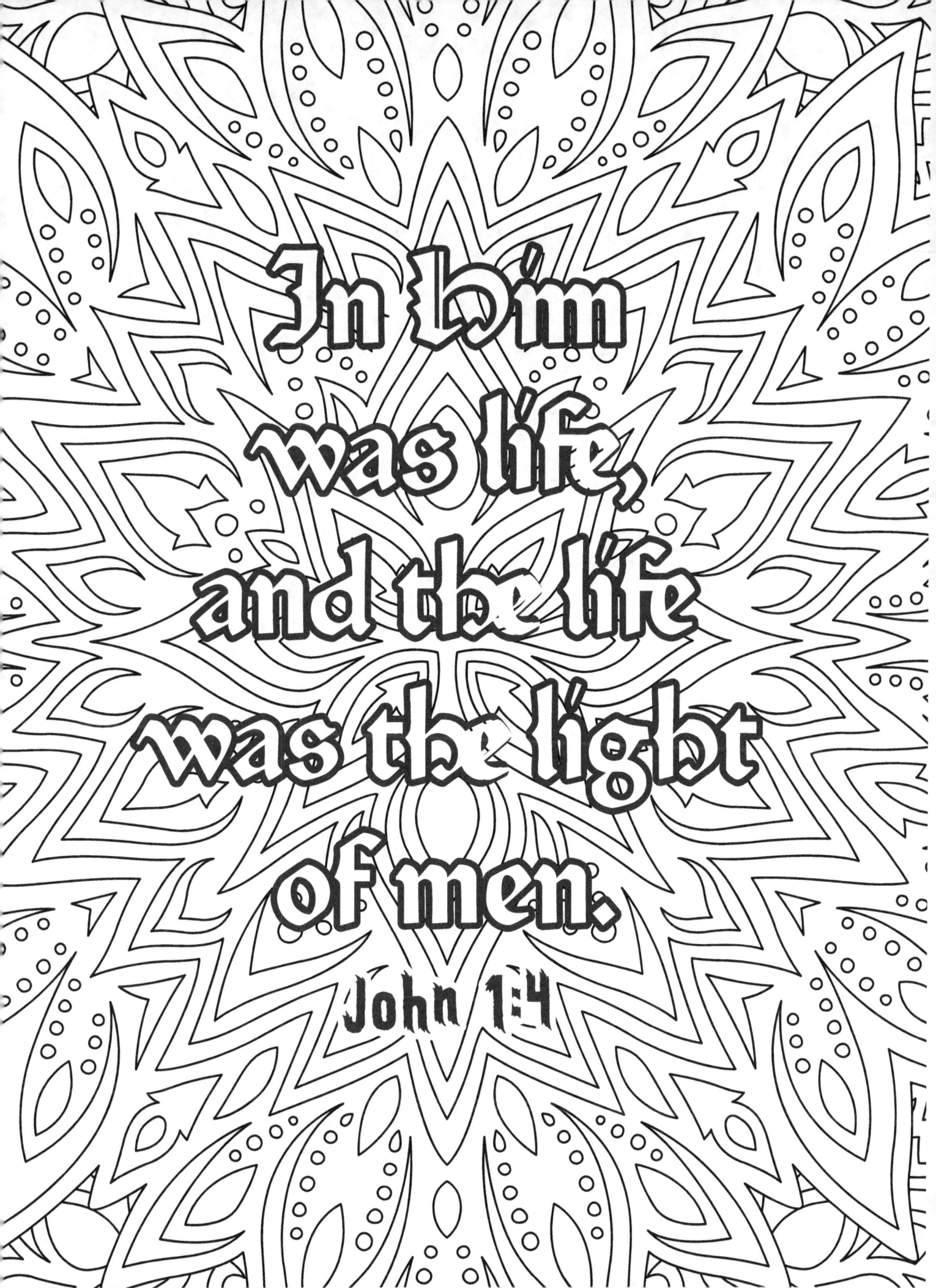

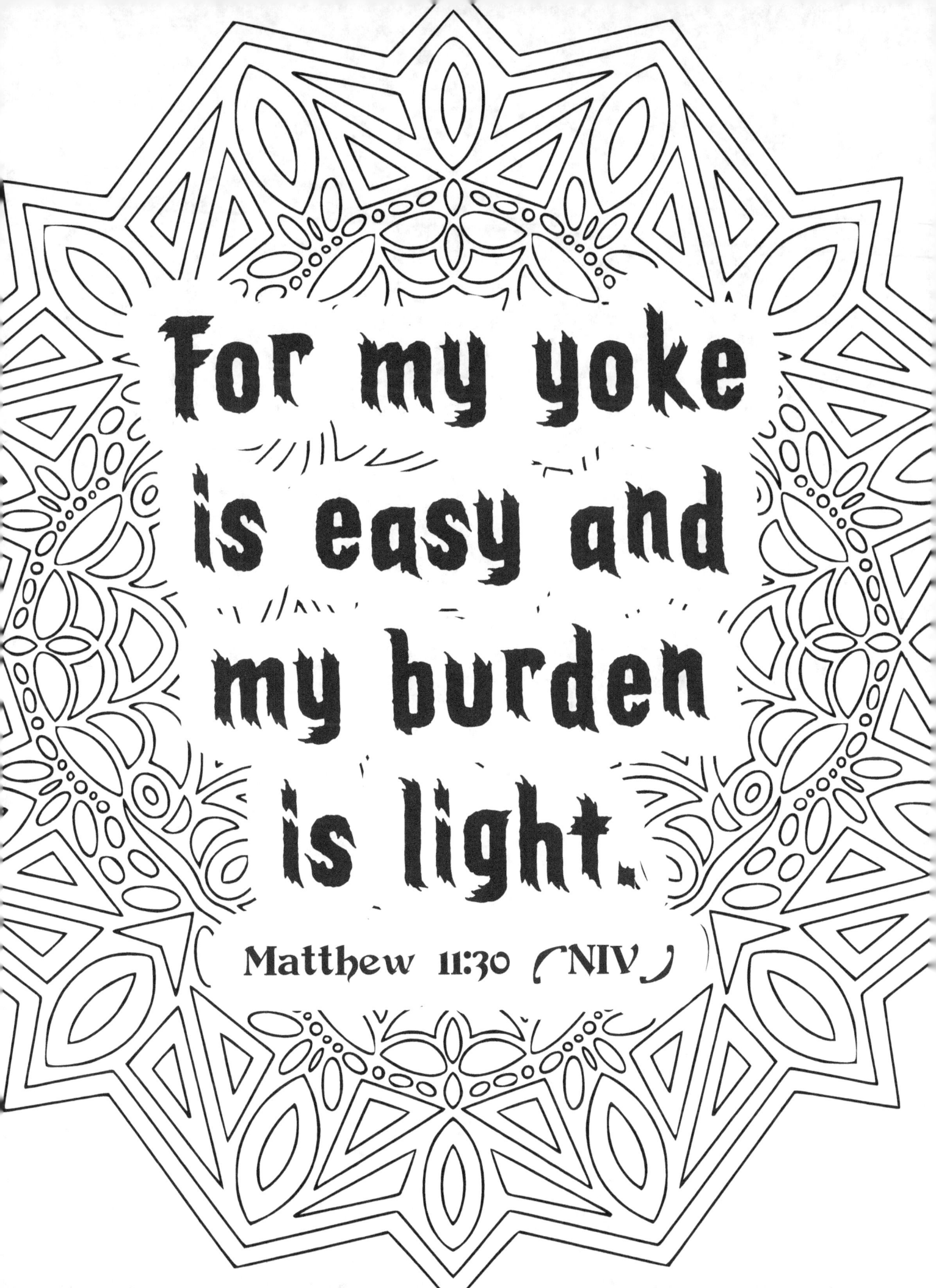

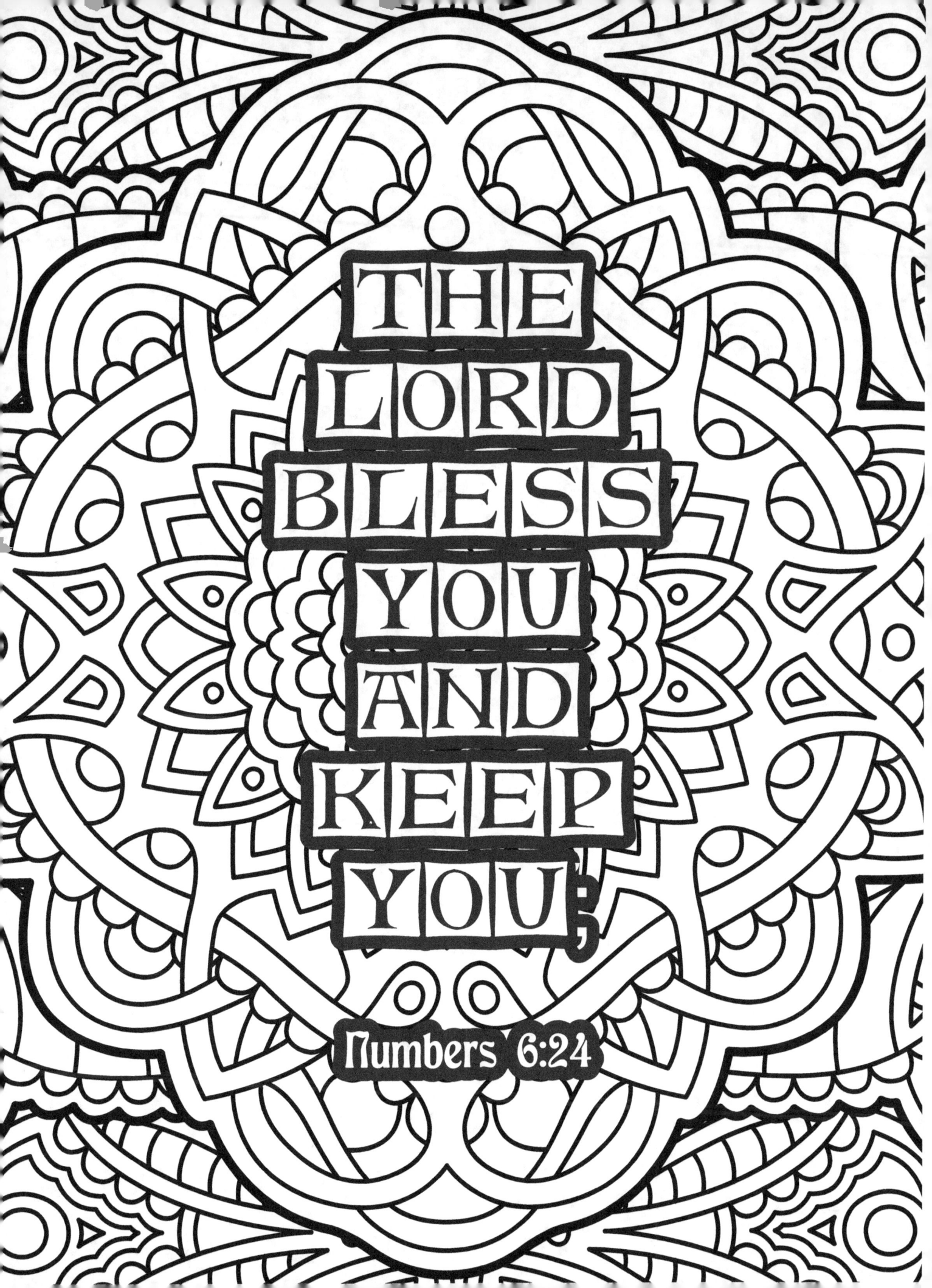

The name of the Lord
is a strong tower;
The righteous run to it
and are safe

Proverbs 18:10

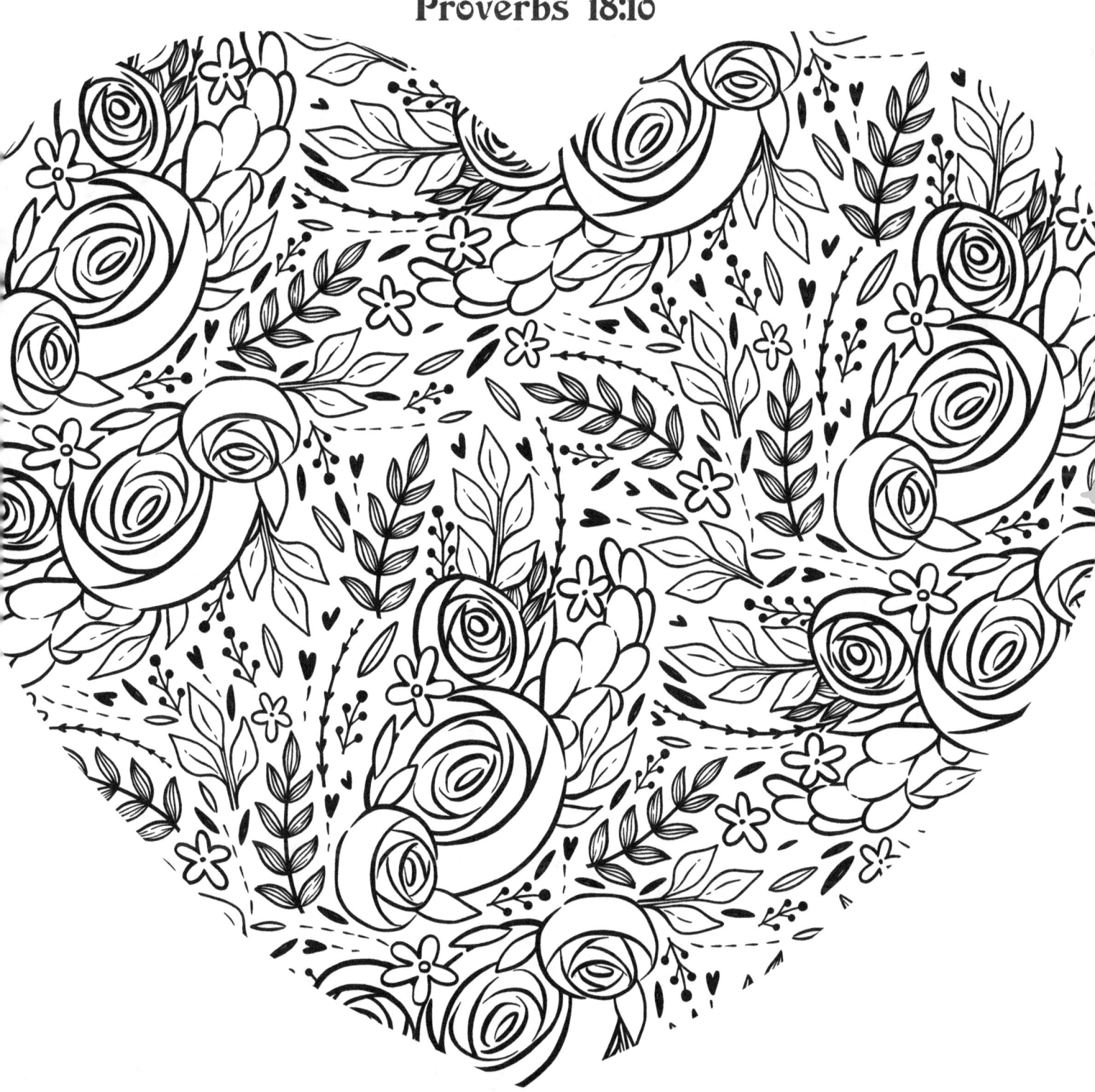

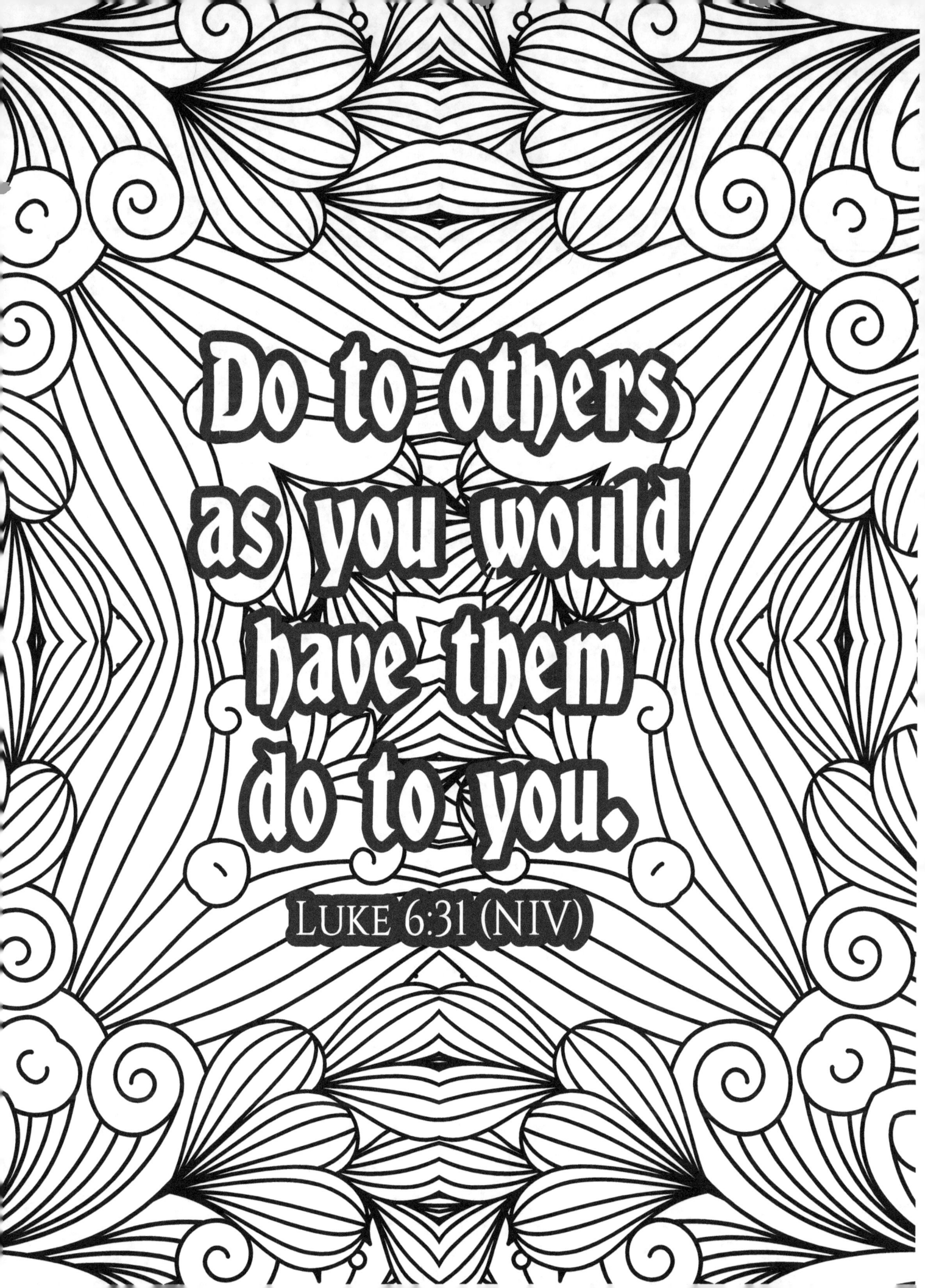

OH, GIVE THANKS TO THE Lord, FOR HE IS good! FOR HIS MERCY ENDURES forever.

PSALM 136:1

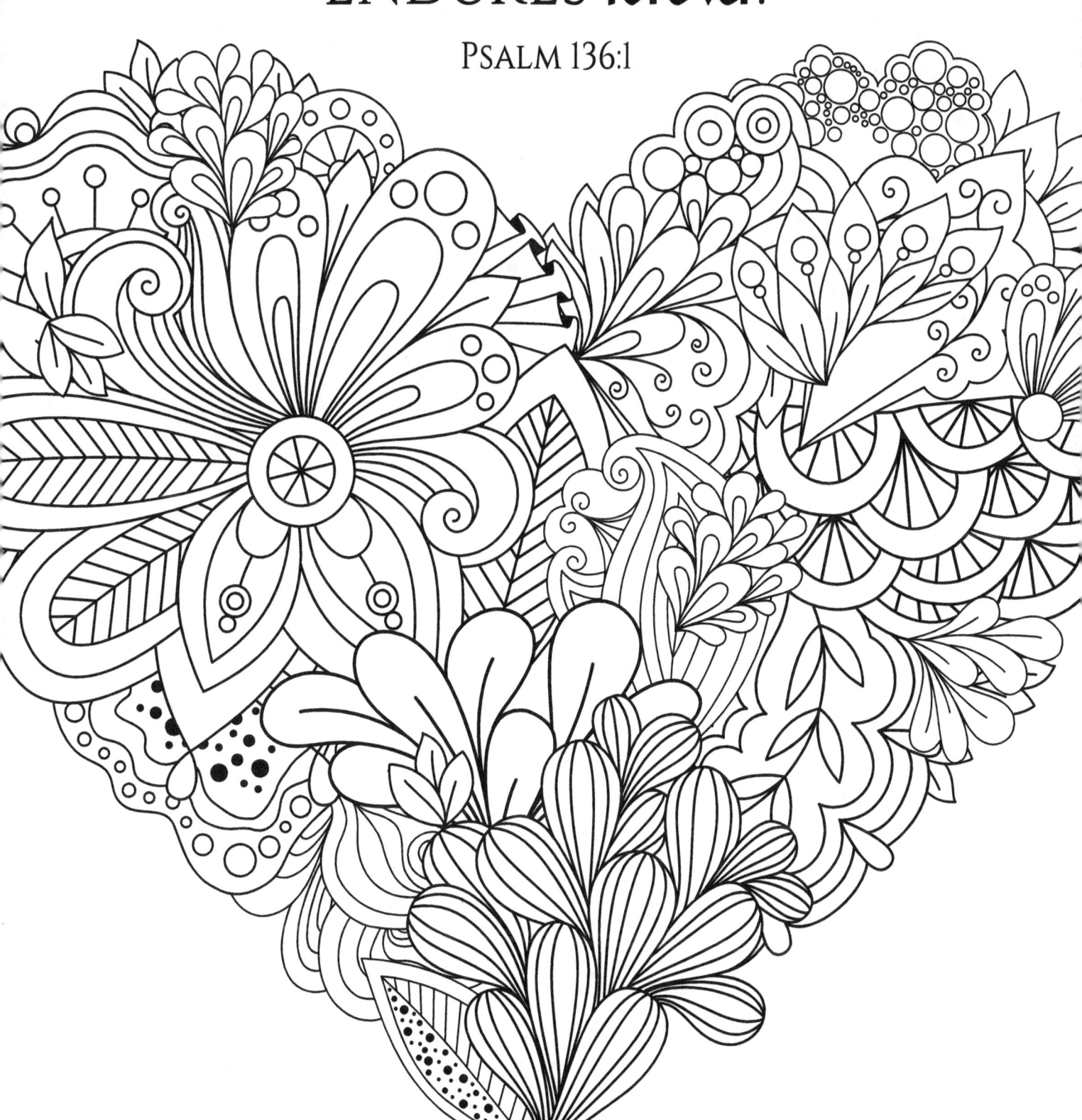

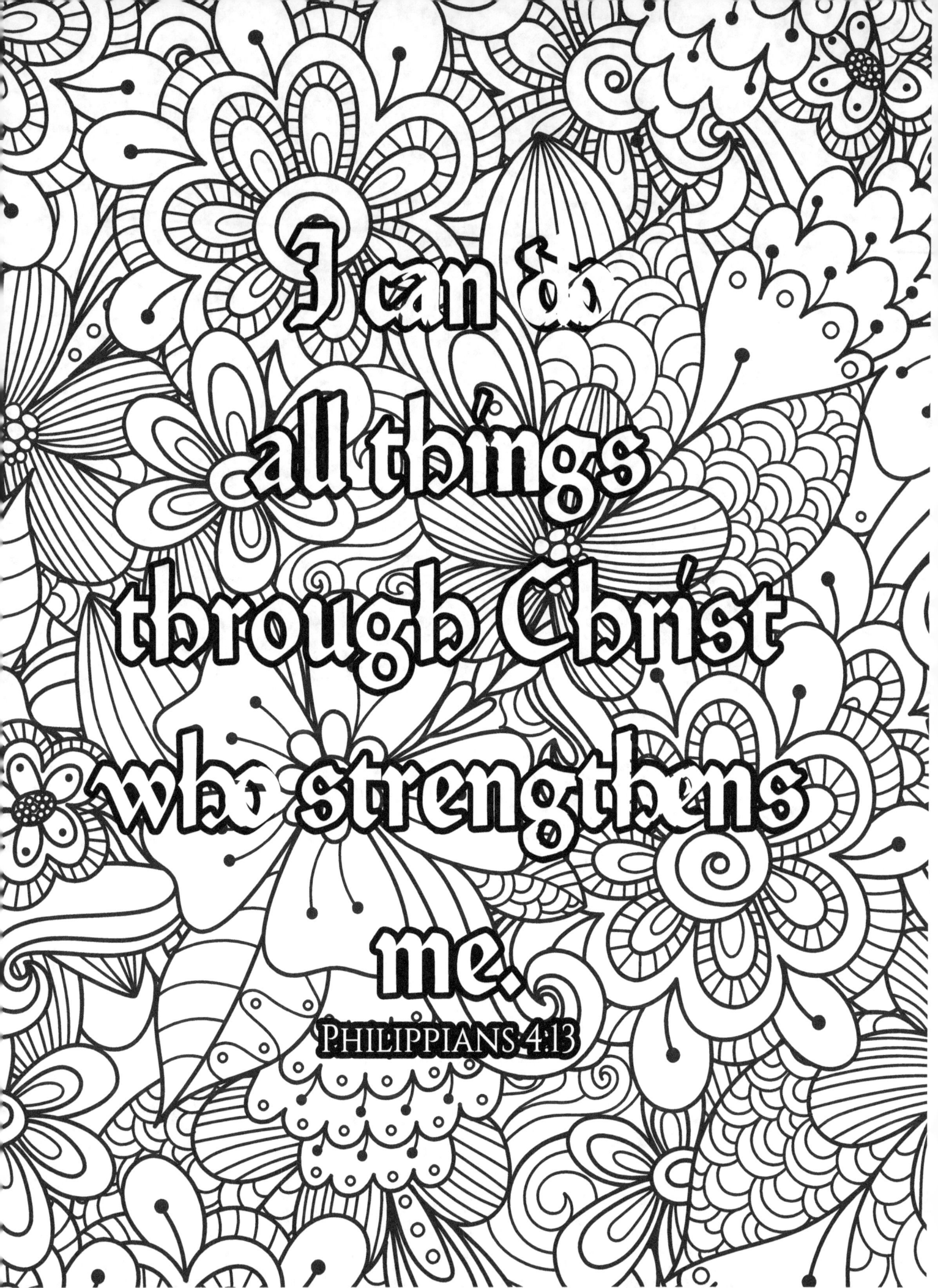

I can do all things through Christ who strengthens me.

PHILIPPIANS 4:13

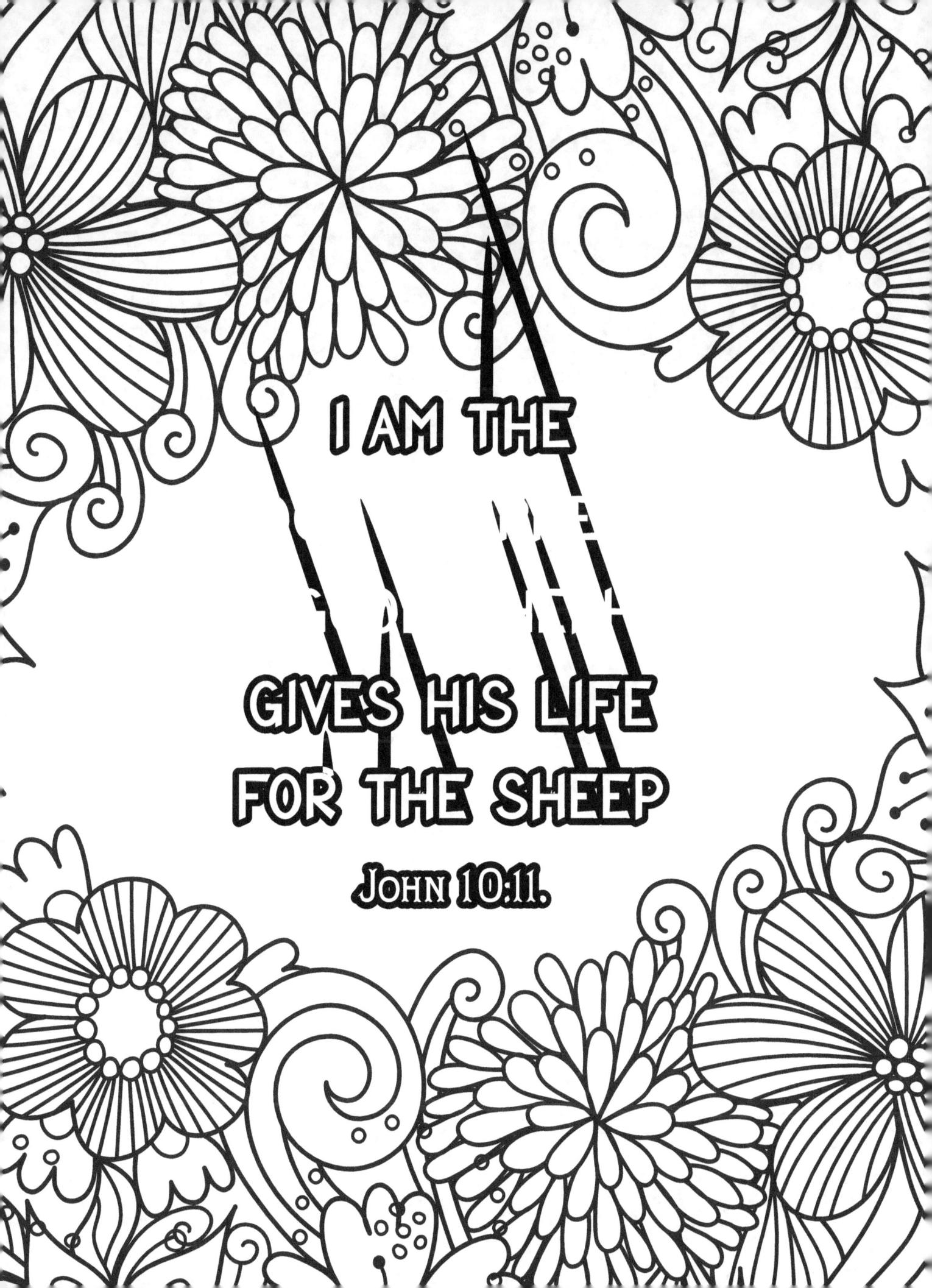

I AM THE

GIVES HIS LIFE
FOR THE SHEEP

John 10:11.

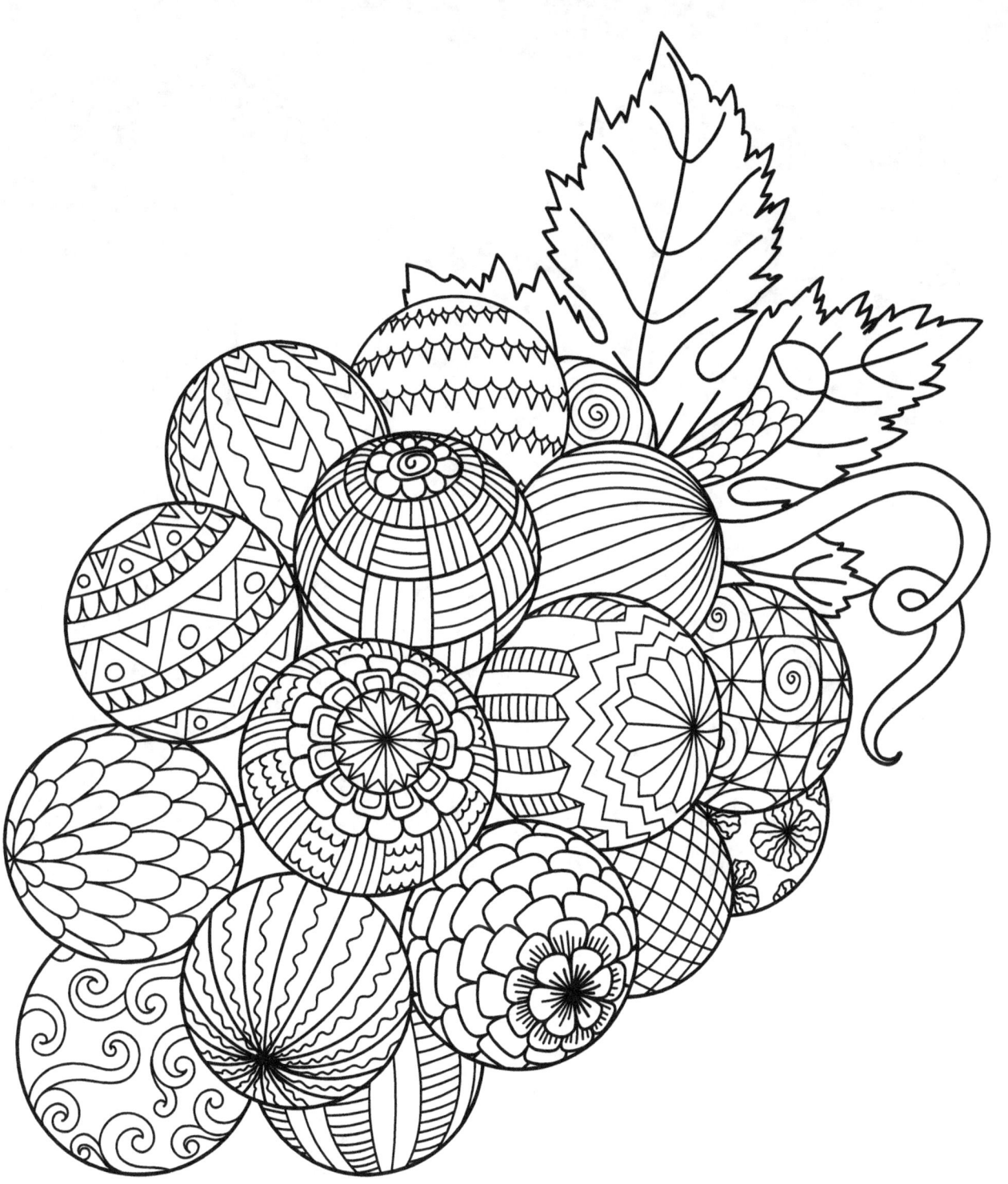

Commit your way to the Lord,
Trust also in Him,
And He shall bring it to pass.

Psalm 37:5

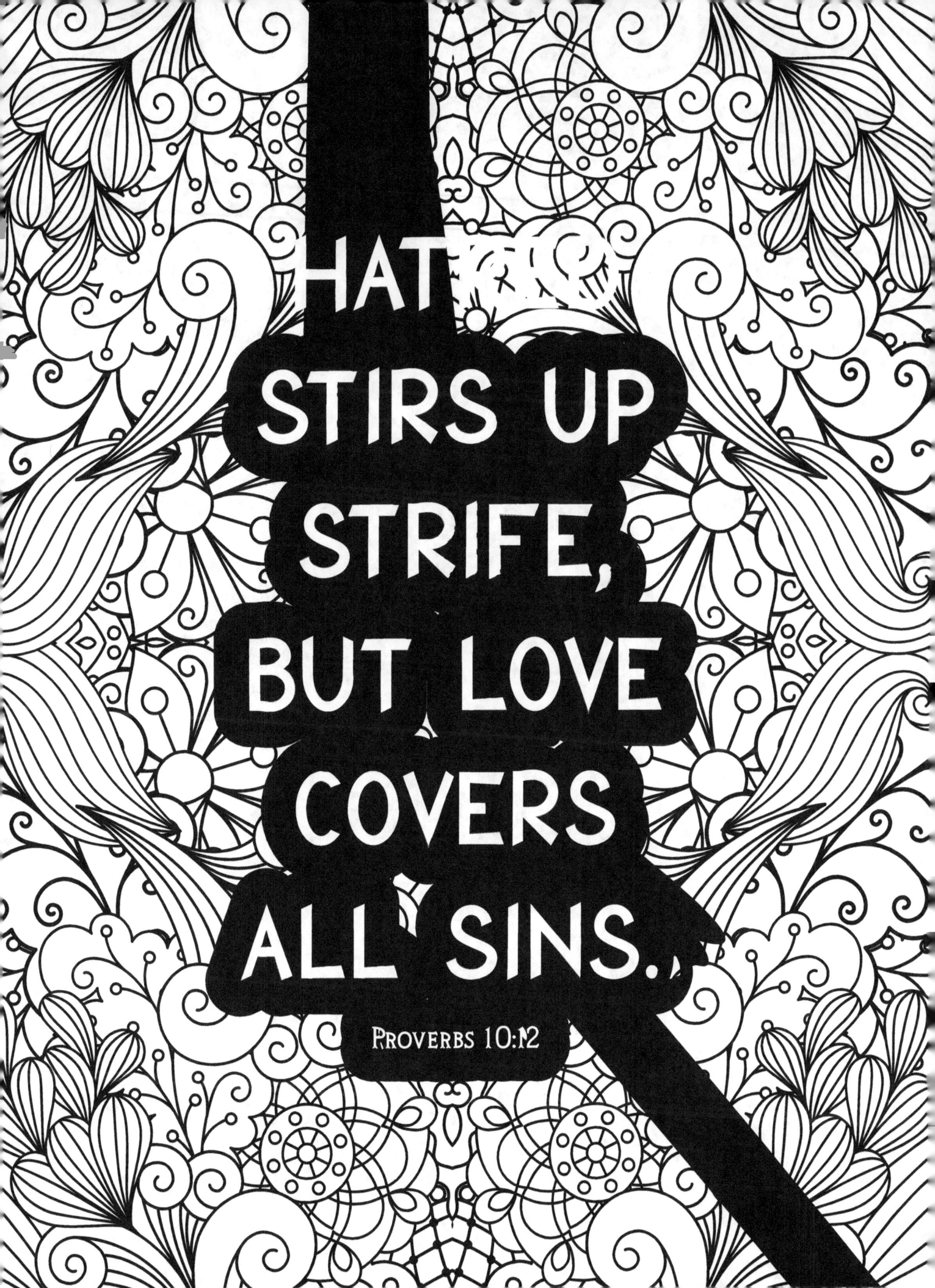

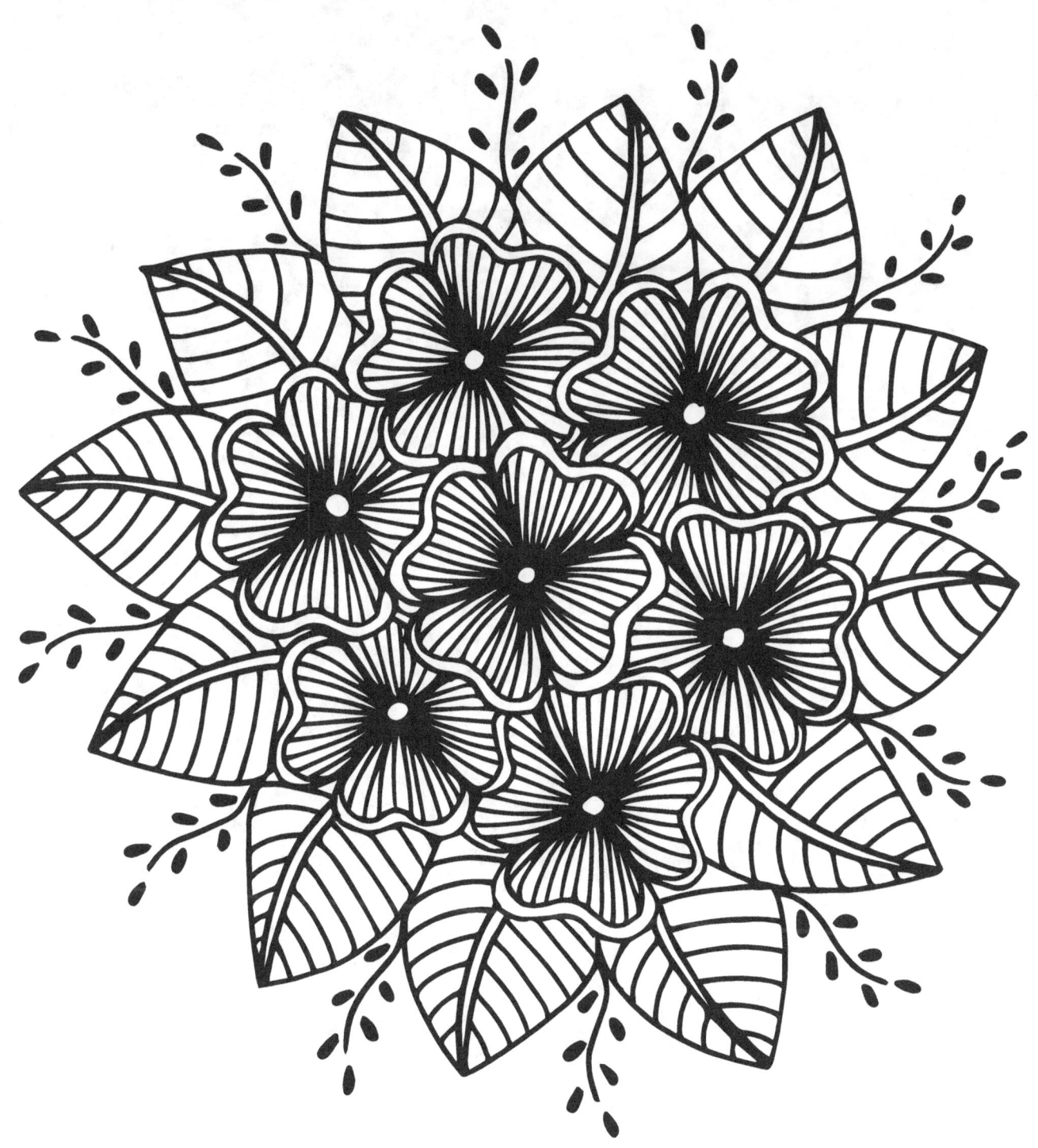

REJOICING IN HOPE,
PATIENT IN TRIBULATION,
CONTINUING STEADFASTLY
IN PRAYER

Romans 12:12

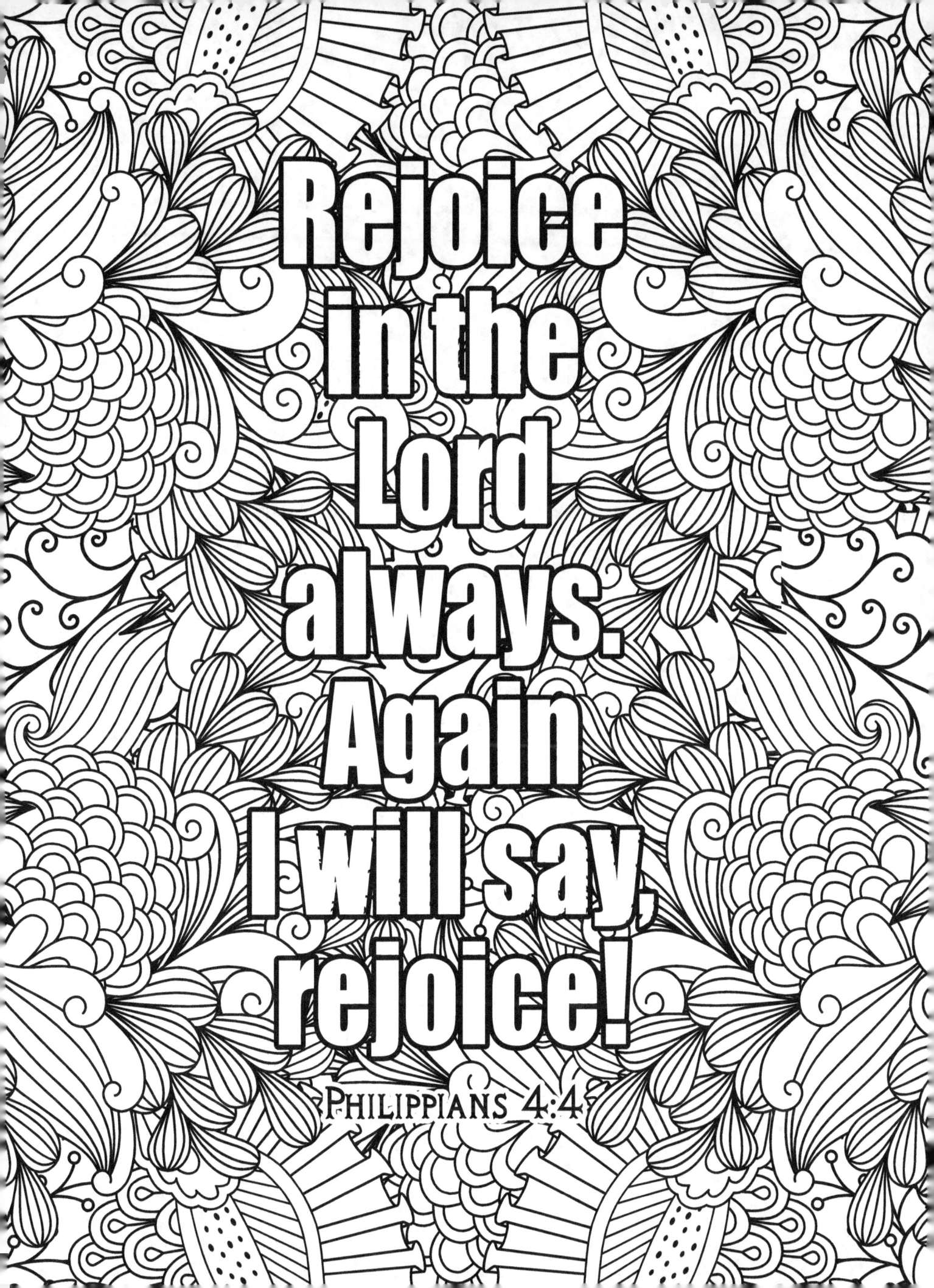

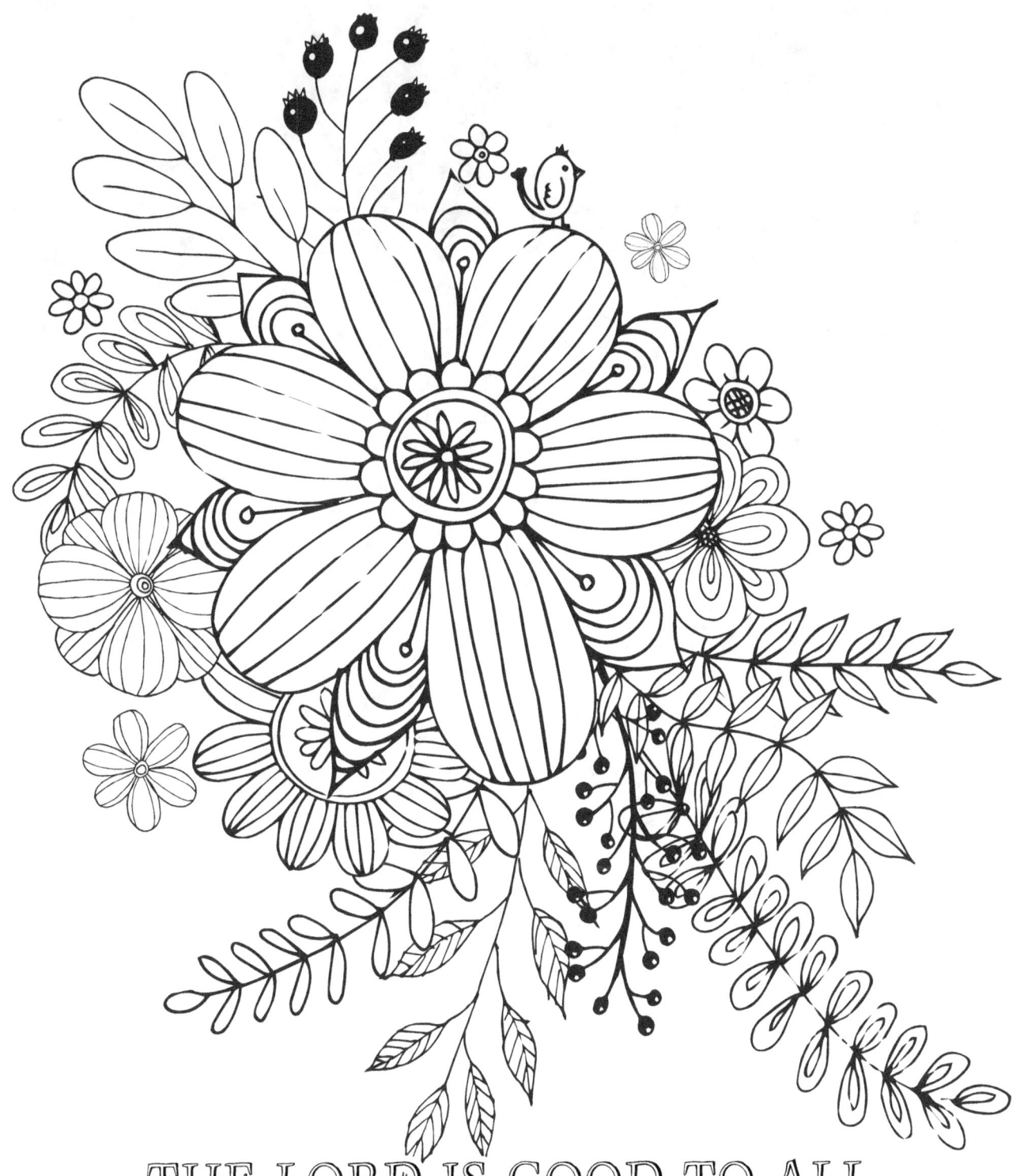

THE LORD IS GOOD TO ALL,
AND HIS TENDER
MERCIES ARE OVER
ALL HIS WORKS.

Psalm 145:9

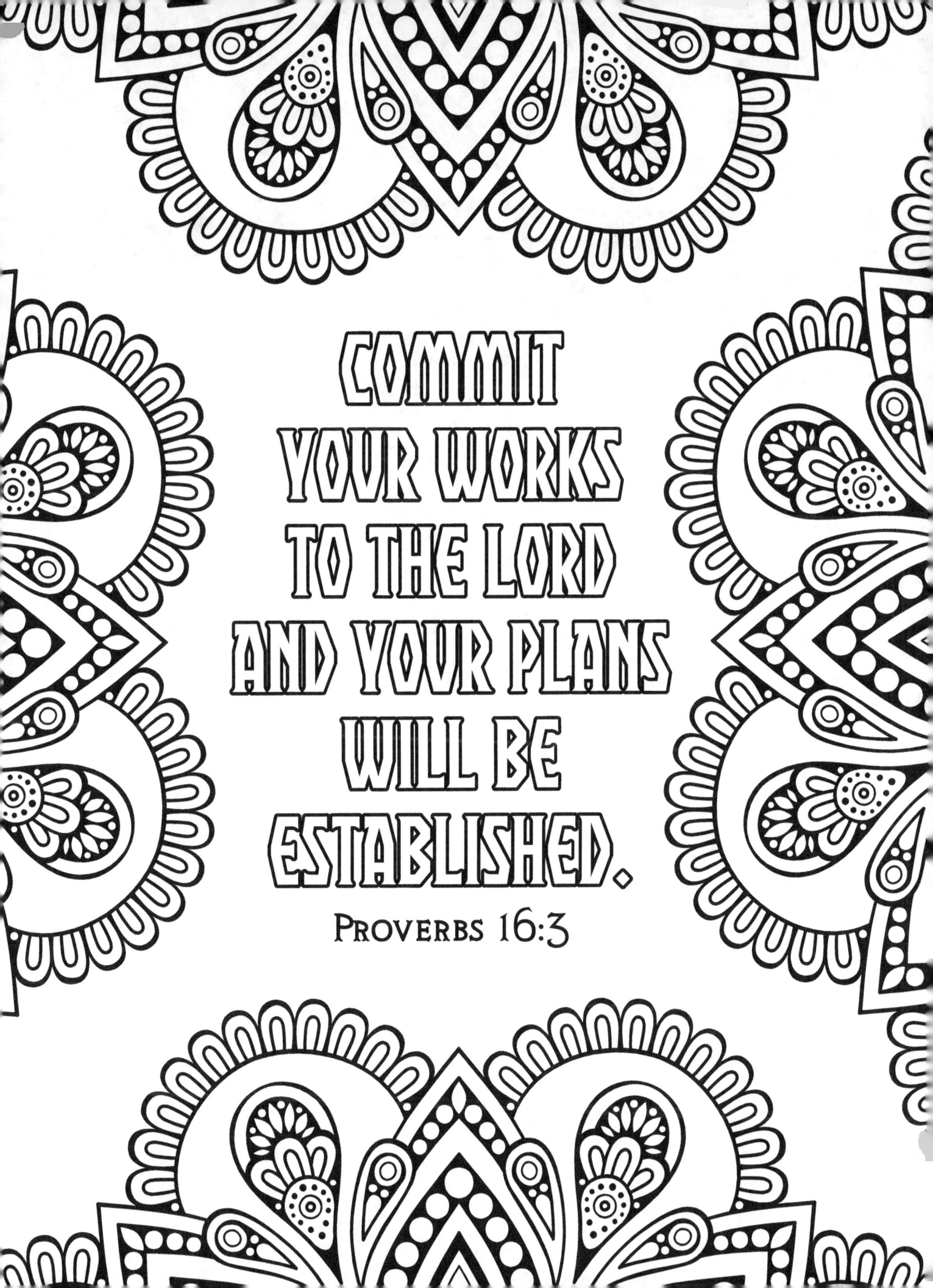

COMMIT YOUR WORKS TO THE LORD AND YOUR PLANS WILL BE ESTABLISHED.

Proverbs 16:3

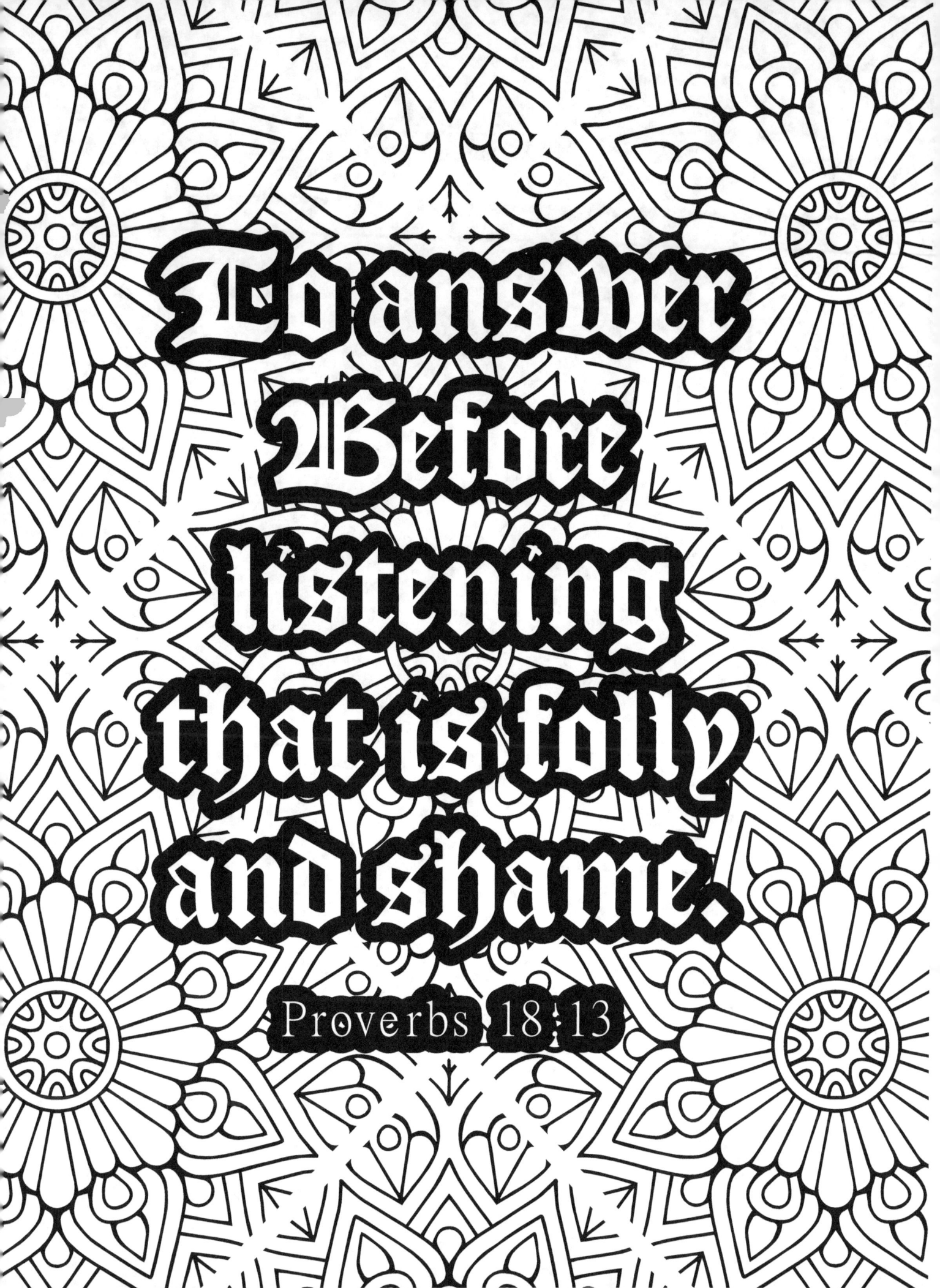

To answer Before listening that is folly and shame.

Proverbs 18:13

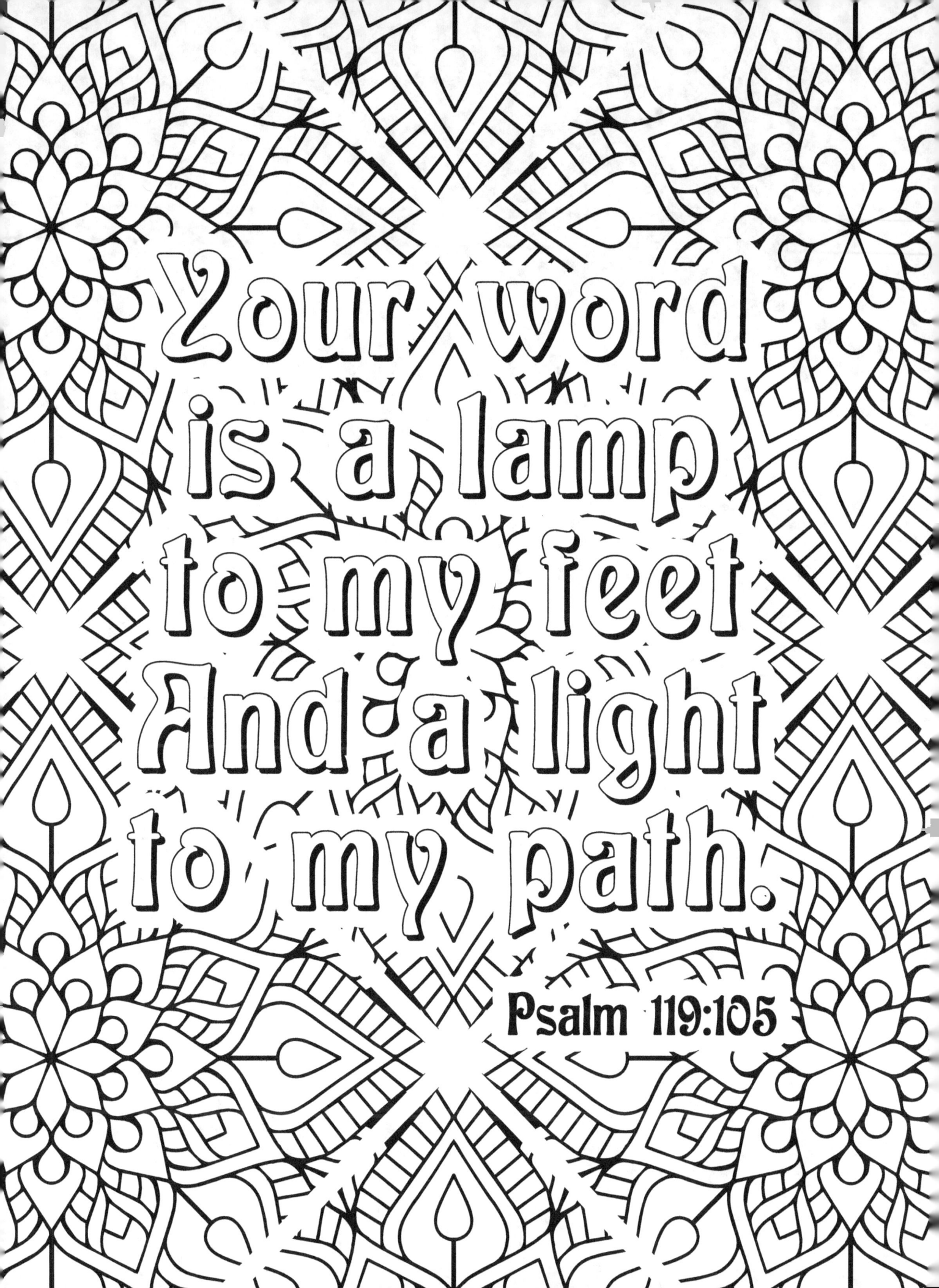

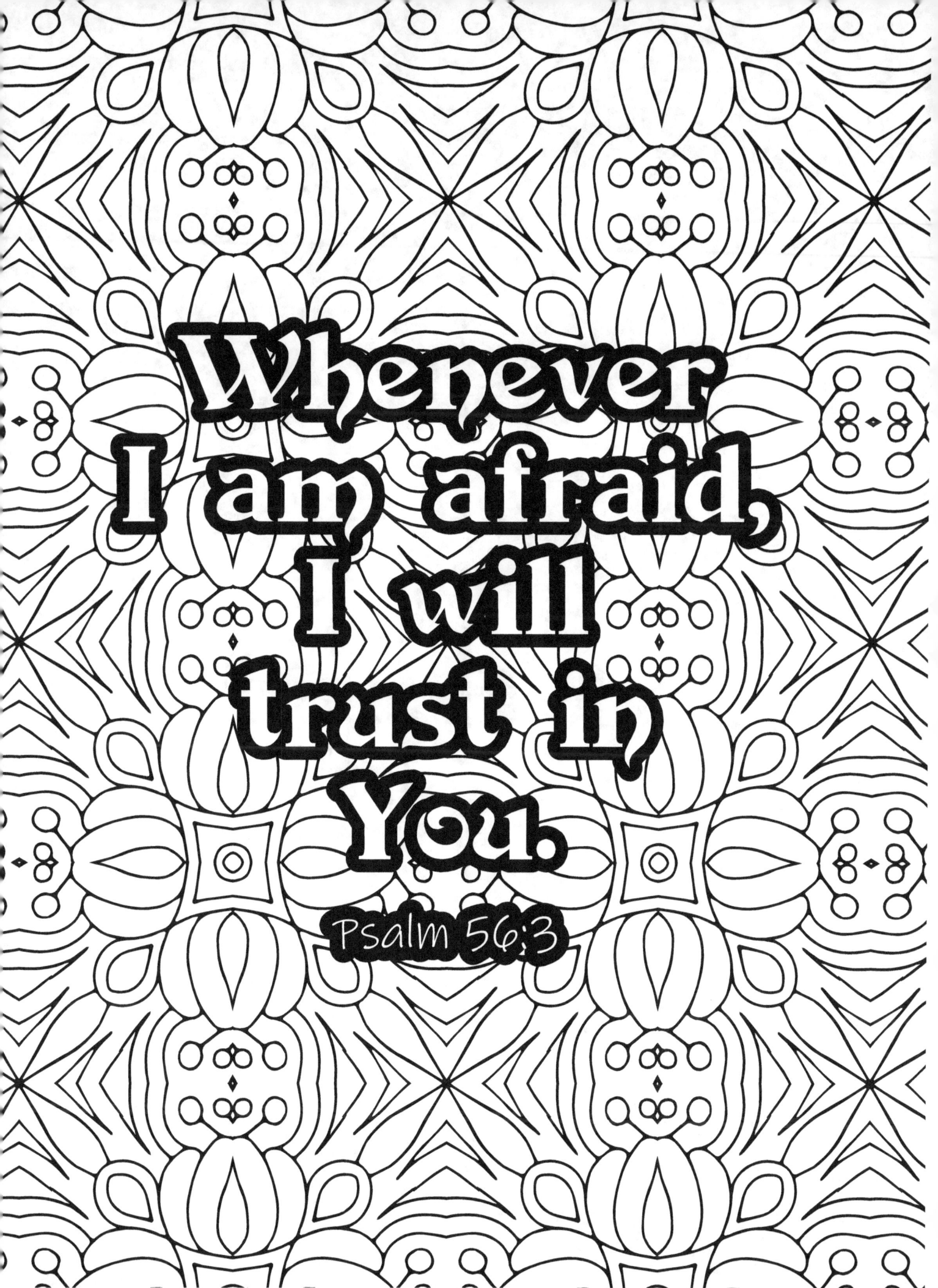

Whenever I am afraid, I will trust in You.

Psalm 56:3

The Lord
is my light
and my
salvation
whom
shall I
∞ fear? ∞

PSALM 27:1

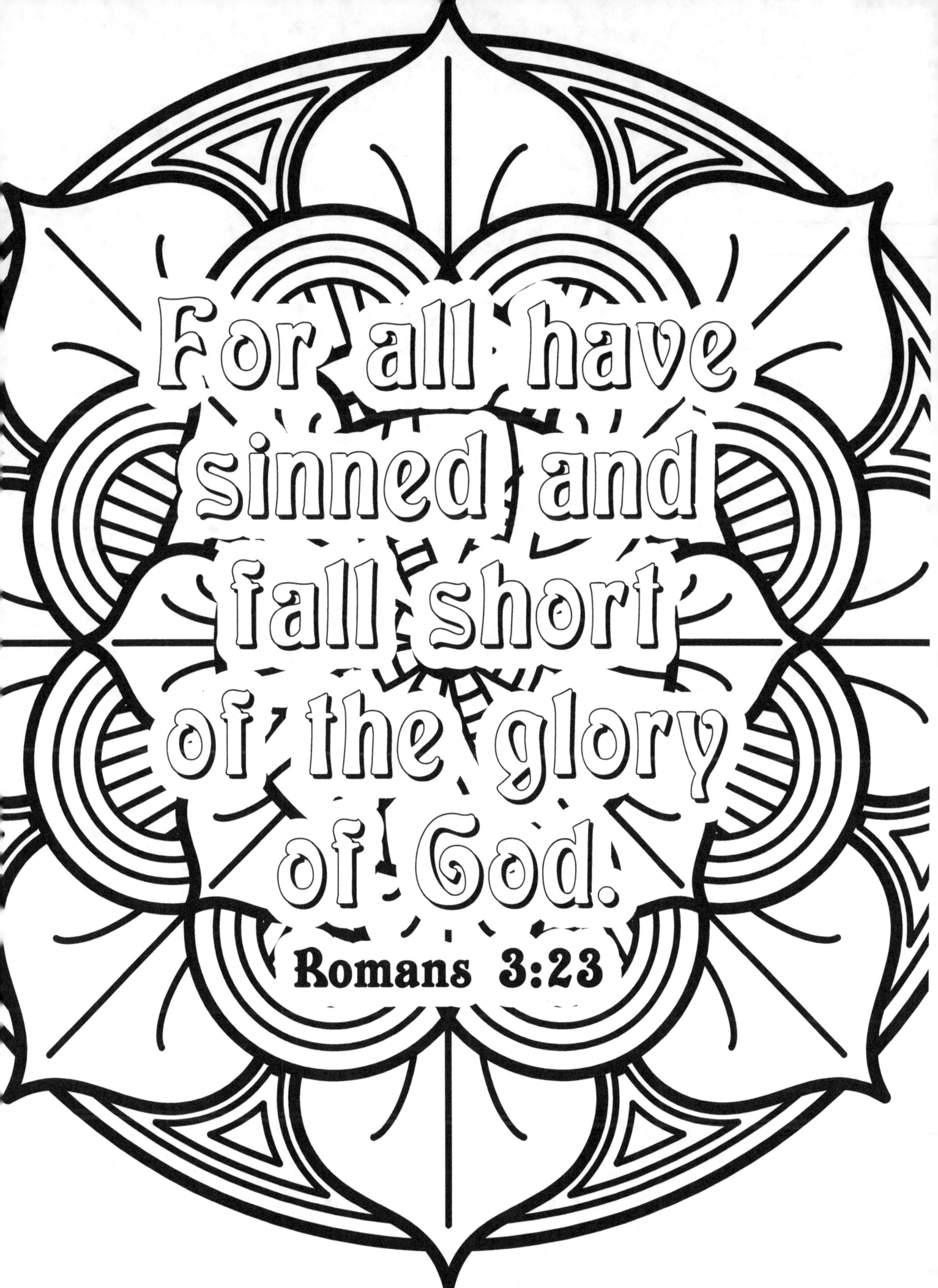

This is the day
the Lord has made;
We will rejoice and be glad in it.
Psalm 118:24

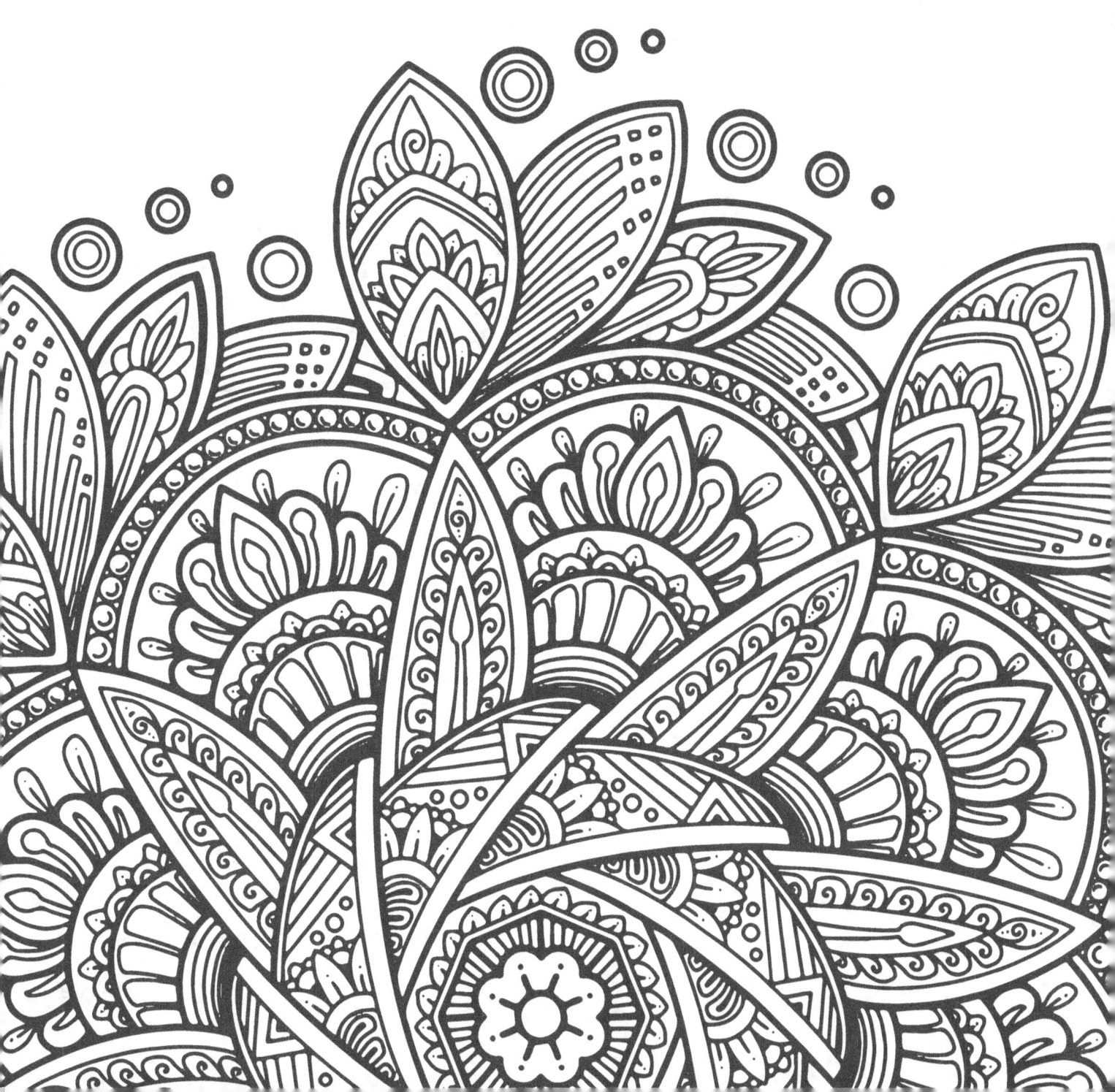

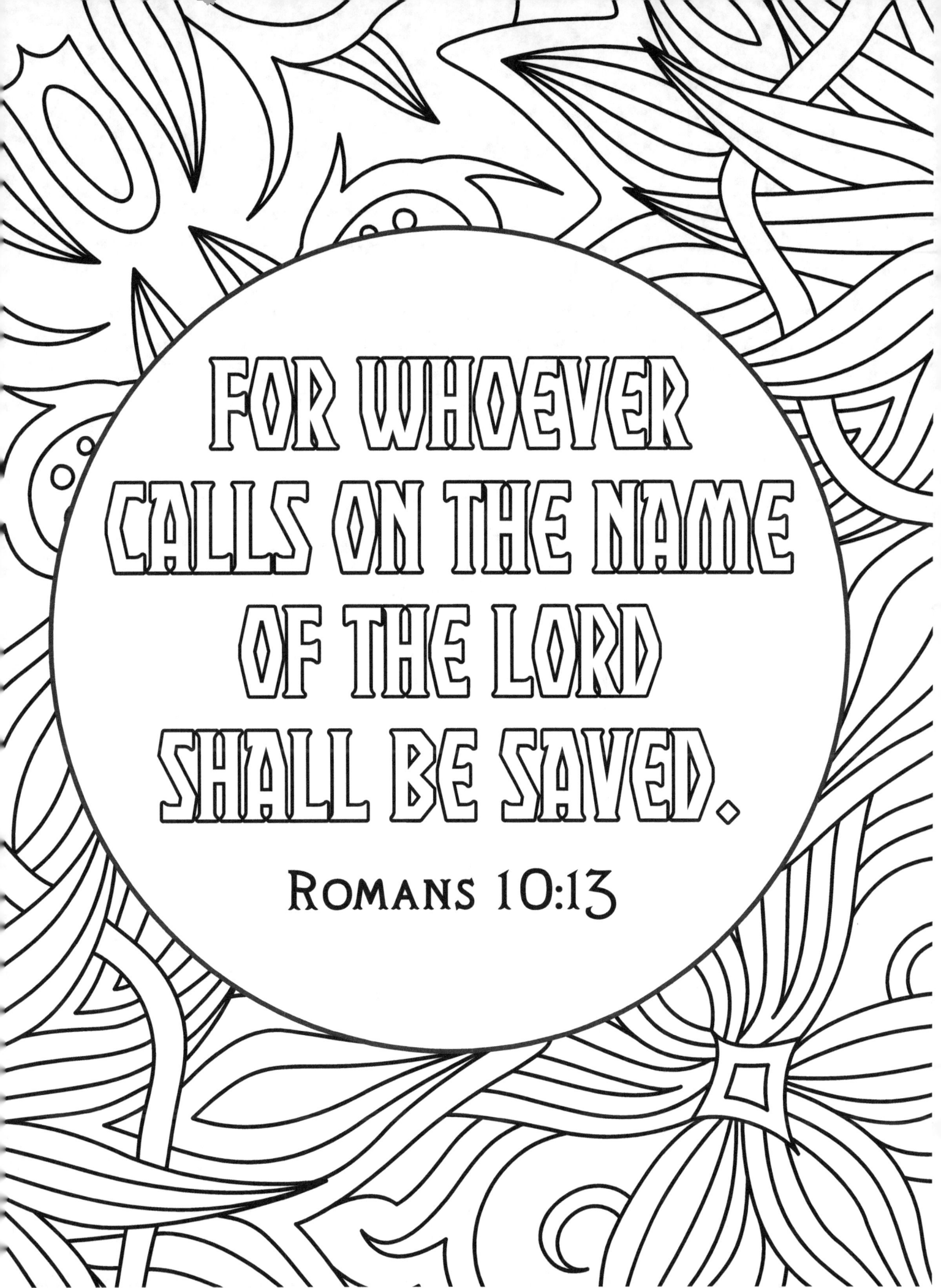

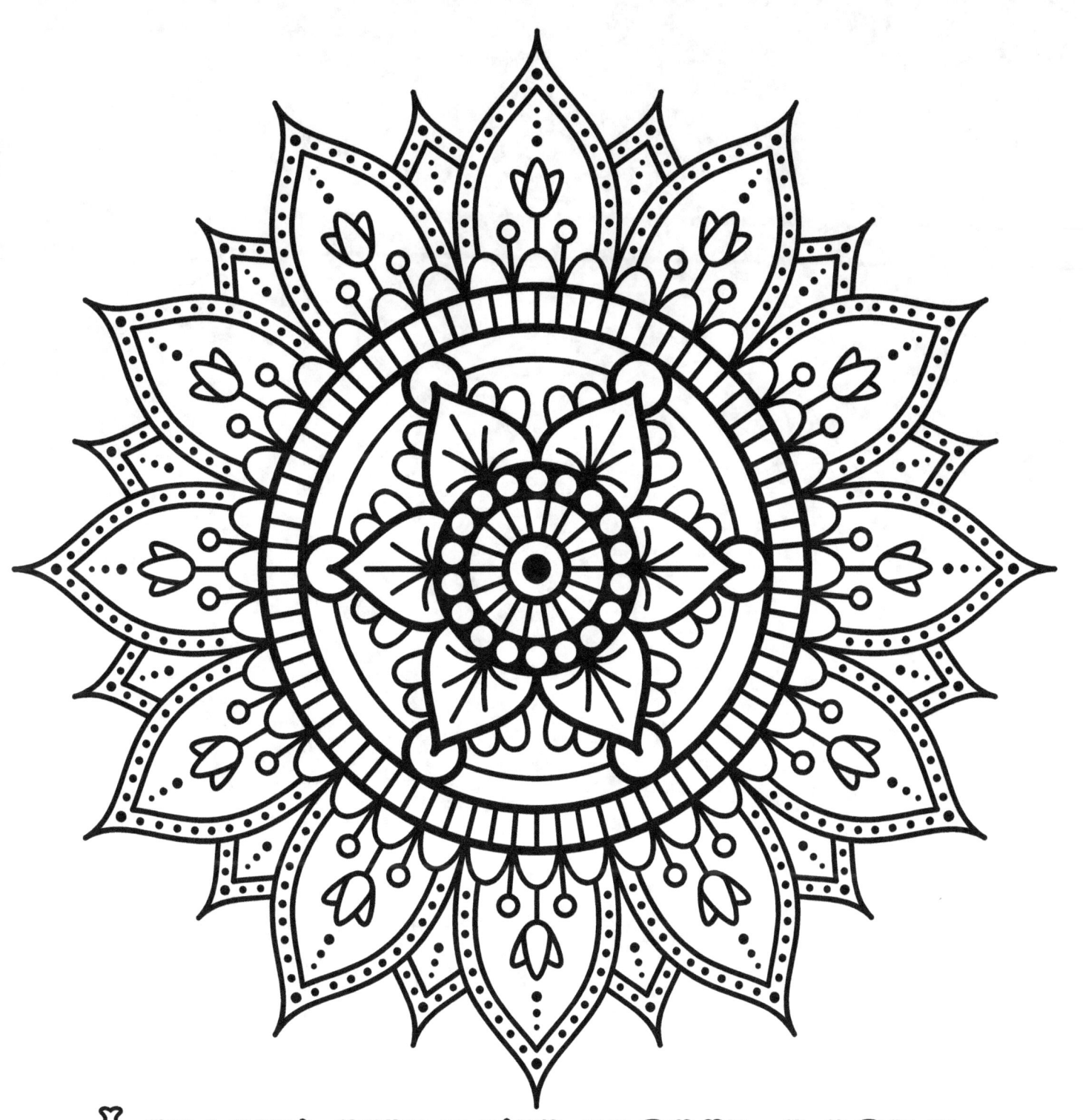

I HAVE HIDDEN YOUR WORD
IN MY HEART
THAT I MIGHT NOT SIN
AGAINST YOU.

Psalm 119:11

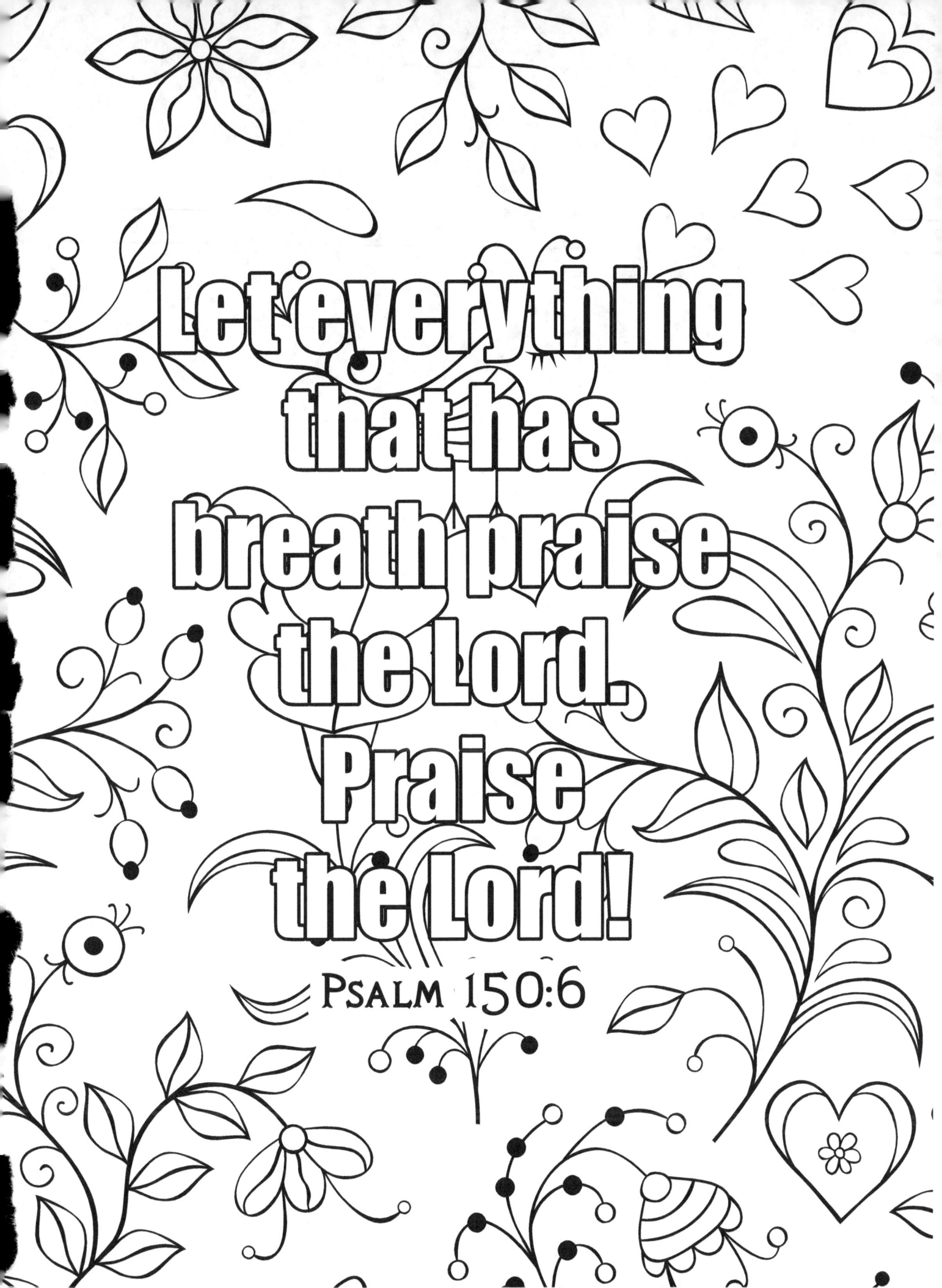